Palgrave Pioneers in Criminology

Series Editors
David Polizzi, Indiana State University, Terre Haute, USA
James Hardie-Bick, School of Law, Politics & Sociology,
University of Sussex, Brighton, UK

Palgrave Pioneers in Criminology examines the theorists and their work that has shaped the discussions and debates in the interdisciplinary, growing field of Criminology, focussing particularly on Critical Criminology. The pioneers range from established to newer academics in Criminology and beyond from other disciplines including Sociology, Psychology, Philosophy and Law. Each book in the series offers an overview of a pioneer and their contribution to the field of Criminology, from the perspective of one author or multiple contributors. The series charts the historical development of key theories and brings discussions up to the present day to consider the past, present and future relevance of these theories for society. This series presents in-depth, engaging, new discussions about this field and the directions that it will continue to grow in.

Aaron Pycroft

René Girard and Criminal Justice

Demythologizing the Victim

Aaron Pycroft
School of Criminology and Criminal
Justice
University of Portsmouth
Portsmouth, UK

ISSN 2946-563X   ISSN 2946-5648   (electronic)
Palgrave Pioneers in Criminology
ISBN 978-3-031-82470-8   ISBN 978-3-031-82471-5   (eBook)
https://doi.org/10.1007/978-3-031-82471-5

This Palgrave Macmillan imprint is published by the registered company Springer Nature Switzerland AG
The registered company address is: Gewerbestrasse 11, 6330 Cham, Switzerland

If disposing of this product, please recycle the paper.

With love and thanks to my beautiful family who give me everything and enable me to be whole, not least through the grace of allowing me to play every day: Nicky, Samuel, Rose, Willow, Freddie, Barnabas, Jamie, Lydia and Rob

Acknowledgements

I would like to thank David Polizzi for inviting me to write and contribute this book to the Pioneers in Criminology series and for his encouragement, support and friendship. I also have to thank him for allowing me to reproduce sections from Pycroft 2018, 2020 which were originally published in the Journal of Theoretical and Philosophical Criminology. Over the last couple of years, Girard seems to have over-dominated my thinking and so most of all I have to thank Nicky, my wife who has to put up with more than her fair share of Girard, Durkheim and complexity theory in everyday conversation.

Contents

CHAPTER 1

Just Another Dead French Theorist?

Abstract This section gives some brief biographical details concerning Girard, and contextualises his work within the broader development of "French theory" and his positionality within structuralist and post-structuralist debates. I make the argument for why his work has the potential for developing a bridge between theory and practice in criminal justice. His relationship with Christianity is discussed as is mine in respect of a phenomenological and hermeneutical approach to analysing and discussing his work.

Keywords Biography · Structuralism · Post-structuralism · Religion · Collective resentment · Christianity · Roman Catholic

René Girard was born in Avignon, France in 1923 and died in Stanford, USA in 2015. He had been the Andrew B. Hammond Professor of French Language, Literature and Civilization at Stanford University since 1981, (Professor Emeritus since 1995) and was elected as one of the 40 *immortels* of the *Académie Française* in 2005. His fellow *immortel* and compatriot at Stanford, Professor Michel Serres, in praising his genius and influence referred to him as "the new Darwin of the human sciences" (https://www.socialsciencespace.com/2015/11/darwin-of-the-human-sciences-rene-girard-1923-2015/). Following the death of Girard, the President of France, François Hollande, said:

A. Pycroft, *René Girard and Criminal Justice*, Palgrave Pioneers in Criminology, https://doi.org/10.1007/978-3-031-82471-5_1

"He was a compelling and passionate intellectual, a scholar of unbounded curiosity, a brilliant theorist and foundational spirit, a teacher and researcher with an uncommon love for going against the tide. René Girard was a free man and a humanist whose work has made its mark on the history of ideas." (https://churchlifejournal.nd.edu/articles/rene-girard-and-the-present-moment/)

To date René Girard can hardly be regarded as a pioneer in academic criminology with respect to its interdisciplinary development and this (as far as I know) is the first book on the work of Girard written specifically for a criminology and victimology audience (certainly in the English language). The lack of attention on his work may not be surprising given Malcolm Bull's (1994) delightfully mimetic observation that during the apotheosis of social theory in the 1970s and 1980s Girard received most attention in his own country and least in the Anglo-Saxon world. At that time, he was relatively unknown outside of France and California reaching number 14 in the magazine *Lire* chart of French intellectuals[1] with Derrida and Baudrillard not reaching the top 40. My argument is of course that Girard has profound insights that challenge our understanding of justice, contemporary problems therein and potential solutions and to encourage readers to engage critically with his work. The work of Girard offers a significant resource for the development of theoretical, theological and philosophical criminology not least in understanding cultural formation and context. Critically his approach enables the fostering of a personal dimension that is essential in understanding our individual responses to justice, ethics, rehabilitation and the limits of punishment. In Pycroft and Bartollas (2022) we argue that there is nothing in criminology per se that lends itself to a meaningful practice of criminal justice beyond "the administrative" (to use Jock Young's pejorative adjective), and Girard's work offers a conceptual and practical bridge from theory to practice. Some of the concepts that Girard covers in depth do of course exist in criminological discourse, for example scapegoating, but without reference to his work which in my view is an oversight as his work adds radically and significantly to the richness and depth of those discussions. Scapegoating is examined in some detail by Dingwall and Hillier (2015), largely drawing on the work of Mary Douglas (1995)

---

[1] Perhaps only the French could devise a hit parade of intellectuals, though of course it's very existence clearly demonstrates the vibrancy of "French theory" during that period.

(see below). Murji (2019) also discusses the concept as essentially func-
tionalist, problematic and difficult to evaluate. However, Girard's work
has started to emerge in social work literature and particularly through
engagement with the psychodynamic aspects of mimesis, complicity and
empowerment e.g. Houston and Swords (2022). In victimology the work
of Girard and particularly the theological and anthropological dynamics
of the victim label and its relationship to forgiveness is engaged with by
van Dijk (2008). All of this existing work serves to demonstrate the need
for a much fuller appreciation of the work of Girard to understand crime,
the meaning of being a victim and culturally how we address these problems and what the consequences of those actions are for notions of justice
and its outcomes.

To understand Girard's thought it is essential to read his core work
and not rely on meta literature *about* him or which seeks to make claims
for him. I do not claim that this book can serve as a comprehensive introduction to his work and my approach is not biographical, and certainly
not intended as a hagiography but rather as a critical exploration of
my understanding of *le systeme Girard* and whether this might be used
and developed generatively in exploring and working with the relationships between theoretical criminology, victimology and the practices of
justice. In particular I am interested in developing an application of theory
to practice that offers us the capacity for self-critique at the individual,
institutional and cultural levels, thus providing us with the resources to
become peacemakers. I will argue that his thought has the potential to
provide us with a powerful heuristic for understanding causes, consequences and truth through his tripartite model of the mimetic nature of
desire, the scapegoat mechanism and the ways in which these are main-
tained through sacred sacrificial archaic religious practices. We have the
advantage of access to Girard's full body of work and the contours of
his intellectual development, and I want to take what I read to be his
maturity of vision in relationship to advances in social science as an under
examined aspect of victimology and criminology. Our understanding of
complex systems is changing the ways in which we view and understand
the reductionism of either structure or agency. Culturally the judicial
trial and execution of Jesus of Nazareth has judicially and religiously
structured our approach to justice and punishment (see e.g. Gorringe,
1996, 2021), and also reveals solutions to the "locked in" and apparently intractable problems caused by punishment as exclusion. Through
understanding and developing processes of forgiveness we can disrupt

the largely unconscious and unseeing mob that equates punishment with justice. It is the lack of forgiveness which is central to the dynamic of the so-called crisis in criminal justice, as forgiveness is the holding open of the space of possibility for people who have been excluded to return to the benefits of society (Pycroft & Bartollas, 2018, 2022). Because we no longer have a mechanism to do this we simply continue to exclude and marginalise people within the community through all the forms of monitoring and surveillance at our disposal. We need liturgies and ceremonies of welcome, forgiveness and hospitality that enable all concerned to realise a new future. Reintegration can never be predicated on the basis of shame, however positively we try to construct it. We see some evidence of this in restorative practices and in some therapeutic treatment communities, but these approaches can never be mainstream as they fundamentally challenge the metaphysical justifications for punishment. Justice is defined as punishment and punishment as justice, despite there being little evidence for satisfaction for any of those involved.

The use of religion for the structuring of collective resentment was well understood by the Masters of Suspicion e.g. Freud, Marx and Nietzsche who (like the evangelical atheists Dawkins, Dennett, etc.) either do not comprehend why the myths of religion continue and/or why they cannot be eradicated. In practice and in relation to the crimes of the powerful and the oppression of people, religion continues to be appropriated by state power to create the necessary scapegoats for the mobilisation of electoral advantage, but at another are a key source of resistance to state power (Žižek, 2009). Victim status, mythically defined is both a source of order and disorder and that status has been variously constructed relative to the movements of history, and the masters of suspicion having expelled God, have replaced Him with their own mythologisation which serves to conceal the violence of theirs and our thoughts and actions.

This book is my reading and interpretation of Girard's work, its promises and limitations with an approach that is phenomenological and hermeneutical in exploring his thought and the ways in which this is incorporated into my own hermeneutical narrative. This represents a continuation and deepening of some of the frameworks articulated in Redemptive Criminology (Pycroft & Bartollas, 2022) and with a particular focus on the victim as a source of both order and disorder. My aim is straightforward; to explore and develop Girardian thought as a basis for peacemaking and transformative justice through an application of Girard's work to my own sense-making within the criminal justice system. My interest in Girard has developed over time in relation to four key areas (1) addictive and compulsive behaviours by individuals, groups and institutions who engage in sub-optimal behaviours that are ultimately destructive of themselves (see e.g. Pycroft, 2010) (2) the limits of reductionism in science and social science and the need to apply the principles of complexity theory and whole systems approaches in criminal justice and social work to understand the person in context (see e.g. Pycroft & Bartollas, 2014) (3) in understanding context the need for criminology to engage with neglected theological and philosophical discourse in sensemaking (see e.g. Pycroft & Bartollas, 2022) (4) within all of the above to make sense of myself through the development of my own hermeneutical narrative in relation to the work that I do. Who I am is not separate from the jobs that I have done in academia and working with vulnerable people with addictions, complex needs and involved with the criminal justice system. Further, when it comes to understanding what informs positive outcomes from interventions it is not the use of punishment and coercion but rather motivation, empathy and confidence building working with and resourcing the self-organising capabilities of each person.

On realising that the theory he had developed was already contained and made explicit in the Judaeo-Christian scriptures Girard as a consequence returned to the Catholic faith that he had not practised since a child. It is argued by James Alison (2017) that Girard saw no contradiction or rivalry between the theological implications of his thought and anthropology. However, he was in a positivist tradition and argued for the importance of empirical evidence that anthropology provides and in this sense is entirely atheistic in his approach (in much the same way that Henri Atlan (2013) argues for an atheistic reading of scripture). Alison (2017: 202) states that the insights,

> ...Girard sets out can be read forwards into an account of secular modernity and backwards into what we learn from much earlier periods, derived from their own accounts. This yields a very dynamic hermeneutic, since it sees nothing in a linear fashion. At any stage of history, any literary artefact, and indeed with much greater difficulty, any artefact at all, can be looked at as a particular trace of where humans have reached in their being structured from within by the scapegoat mechanism, with all the many, and entirely unexpected collateral discoveries, which have themselves, enriched a feedback loop to other discoveries.

Like Girard, I am a Roman Catholic[2] and choose to remain a member of that church and grapple with the challenges therein on the basis of a rational exploration of the revelation contained in the Judaeo-Christian scriptures and traditions (see also Pycroft & Bartollas, 2022). Hopefully, this will not be seen as a naive fideism but rather a genuine attempt to engage with what is ontologically real about myself in relation to others and the contexts in which I live and work, evaluated ultimately on the *logos* of the argument presented and its quality. Cynthia Haven (2018: 201) recounts a story of the social and political philosopher Jean-Pierre Dupuy attending a conference and being asked "Why did you become a Girardian?" His answer was "Because it's cheaper than psychoanalysis". Likewise, after a conference presentation where I was exploring approaches to forgiveness in criminal justice, a participant stood up, pointed at me, and asked in an accusatory manner "Are you a Girardian?" My rather more prosaic response then as now is that that Girard provides us with some incredibly useful tools to develop our understanding of the relationships between human nature, violence and religion, and how these relate to practices in addressing crime, punishment, rehabilitation and working in the institutions of justice.

Building on the work of Girard I am convinced that there is an opportunity in criminology to blaze a trail of interdisciplinary work that overcomes the perception of two cultures divide between humanities and science. Increasingly crime science based on biology, chemistry and physics is being taught alongside the more critically oriented criminology in joint honours programmes but with little consideration of why, how or whether they fit together. There is a need to balance

---

[2] "Roman Catholic" is at best an oxymoron as the meaning of "catholic" is "universal" but which is then qualified by "Roman". My position is that of the Second Vatican Council (1962–1965) that the fullness of truth resides in the Catholic tradition. The reason for this is that despite the many historical and ongoing crimes of the institutional church its founding sacrifice, namely the innocent murder victim, Jesus of Nazareth, is a forgiving victim. He does not engage in reciprocal violence and neither do his early followers. This foundational truth, the initial conditions of the church means that it is the only tradition that can genuinely correct itself. This however can never be triumphalist, or taken for granted and is always a gift for others and in Girardian terms is not predicated upon membership of that church or necessarily having any faith at all. In this sense Christianity as leaven leads to the decline of religion, the subversion and ending of sacrifice and finding ultimately that the home of God is among humanity. We are presented with an anthropology rather than metaphysic of soteriology whereby peacemaking relationships are not institutionally defined and bounded.

a syncretic biopsychosocial approach to understanding people with a conceptual grasp of what it means to be authentically human rather than assuming a consensus over a nihilist core to a mechano-cartesian humanity. We can look to the example of Girard in pioneering new modes of thinking, teaching and acting. While Girard refused to be categorised as a structuralist, nonetheless the search for meta-narrative, and the need for interdisciplinary working between science, social science and humanities are key themes of his work. Girard's work evolves, starting with literary theory, then anthropology and finally theology. What develops is a perspective that provocatively articulates an anthropological site of violent human origins, concealed in myths but revealed through, the Judaeo-Christian scriptures. These scriptures constitute anti-myth and provide the hermeneutical key to unlock the truth of human violence and forgiveness. In decoding human desire and violence Girard occupies an interesting space in the humanities and social sciences. His approach sits in a creative space somewhere between structuralism and post-structuralism, with the former representing consciously free, enlightened (conscious) individuals engaged in developing institutions based on language and social contracts, and the latter the death (unconsciousness) of the human subject (see Dupuy & Anspach, 1994). In Isaiah Berlin's differentiation between Hedgehogs and Foxes with the former knowing a lot of little things and the latter, one big thing, then René Girard is a Fox whose one big thing is mimetic theory. He states,

> I stand by these days of debate as a man of few ideas, so simple in their principle that perhaps they amount to no more than a single idea. It would in that case qualify as an '*idée fixe*'. The suggestion has been made... (Girard, 2023: 21)

In the swathe of Nineteenth and Twentieth Century "French theory" René Girard stands out as someone who over the course of his lifetime, provocatively and relentlessly flew in the face of established academic convention. This book seeks to assert that criminologists should view him as not just another dead French theorist among many in the crowded cemetery of structuralism and post-structuralism but as someone whose thought is a rich resource for integrating theoretical criminology and the practices of criminal justice.

Two Cultures in Criminology?

Abstract This section will explore Girard's work within the context of the "Two Cultures" debate between the arts and humanities and science, and the ways in which Girard over the course of his career seeks to not just bridge the divide but argues that it is artificial.

Keywords Two cultures · Creativity · Descartes · Fragmentation of thought · Wholeness · The Johns Hopkins symposium · The Stanford Symposium

An analysis of myth, the death of God discourse, and the meaning of rationality and consciousness are the historical meat (the carnival) that Girard engages with, revealing the nihilism at the heart of reductionism whether espoused by scientific atheists of modernity or the deconstructionists of post modernity. It is interesting then to locate these arguments within the two cultures debate concerning the relationships and perceived divide between "science" and the "arts" which became infamous in the early 1960s. This debate was in itself a further expression of culture wars and the two cities thesis (*Civitas Dei* and *Civitas Mundi*) instigated when Tertullian in the third century CE asked the question:

> "...what does Jerusalem have to do with Athens, the Church with the Academy, the Christian with the heretic? Our principles come from the

9

A. Pycroft, *René Girard and Criminal Justice*, Palgrave Pioneers in Criminology, https://doi.org/10.1007/978-3-031-82471-5_2

Porch of Solomon, who himself taught that the Lord is to be found in simplicity of heart. I have no use for a Stoic or a Platonic or a dialectic (i.e. Aristotelian) Christianity. After Jesus Christ we have no need of speculation, after the Gospel, no need of research. Once we come to believe, we have no desire to believe anything else; for the first article of our faith is that there is nothing else we have to believe" (Prescriptions against Heretics 7 cited by Wolterstorff, 1999:4)

An exploration of the two cultures debate provides us with a useful framework to explore aspirations for human flourishing (economic and cultural) and the development of language for collective action in promoting, ensuring and maintaining that flourishing against the backdrop of human violence, blame and responsibility in Girard's thought which he argued are revealed initially through reading great literature (e.g. Shakespeare, Cervantes, Dostoevsky, Proust) but likewise realised were already revealed in the Judaeo-Christian mythos. He was starting his career in the post war period and by the 1960s the "white heat of technology" that was to drive the post war boom saw the ascendancy of science and technology over the arts and humanities. The intellectual world was given notice of this ascendancy when in 1959 Sir Charles Snow delivered the Rede Lecture at Cambridge University entitled "Two Cultures and the Scientific Revolution" in which he argued that it was science and technology that could best meet humanity's fundamental needs. But, he argued, this goal was being frustrated by the ignorance between the two cultures. He said that scientists had "the future in their bones" while literary critics were "natural Luddites". Snow was seen to speak with some authority as he had been both a research scientist and also a successful author. The lecture promoted a great deal of popular discussion and following his election victory in 1964 the then Prime Minister, Harold Wilson invited Snow to become a Minister in the newly created Ministry of Technology. The term "administrative criminology" was coined by Jock Young to describe positivist research in the British Home Office that was emerging during this period and culminating in Martinson's "nothing works" research (Martinson, 1974). This new approach was to reduce opportunities for offending, while incarcerating those who did offend. The role of criminologists was to evaluate the effectiveness of those approaches. Young describes these approaches as "A detachment of individuals from the social structure, a denial of history, a loss of meaning; it forgoes transformative politics and concentrates on amelioration and accommodation to the status quo" (Young, 2012: 427). In 1962 the literary critic and Cambridge Don, F.R Leavis was selected by the students to deliver the Richmond Lecture at Downing College Cambridge, and he used the opportunity to deliver an excoriating attack on Snow, both personally and professionally. Leavis was criticised for bad manners (very un-English!) which drew the focus of attention and unfortunately had the effect of eliding some of the key criticisms that he was making about the two cultures argument. Bad manners aside, for Leavis creativity is at the core of what it means to be human as expressed in a congruence between reality and thought, with thought only being possible through language. The most advanced use of language was to be found in the great writers who were able to convey rather than simply express feeling: "'Thought', then, was not a matter of finding words to express independently-existing ideas, but of building upon the living language to forge new ideas. To put it another way, for Leavis thought was an act of creation rather than discovery – it was the extension of the shared human conscious-ness embodied in language" (Ortolano, 2005: 7 emphasis retained). The focus for Leavis is the ways in which the enlightenment reification of science following Newton and Descartes and its reductionism destroys the language of shared human consciousness. Language is now used to describe rather than create, and language itself is seen as problematic e.g. background noise that gets in the way of scientific method and reduc-tive interpretation. Whatever the merits of the arguments between Snow and Leavis, the focus for Leavis was not one of being anti-science, but a concern for culture and civilisation as a consequence of reductionist thinking. Reading Leavis the similarity with the quantum physicist David Bohm is striking. Bohm argues (2000) that our world view is based upon a confusion whereby, because we think reductively, we assume that the world is fragmented rather than us seeing the ontological reality of undi-vided wholeness. The problem becomes one of how we both see and give creative expression to that undivided wholeness that is in flowing movement. Likewise, for Leavis: "The disease of modern civilisation was the mental distinction between words and things, language and reality, communication and experience...the point to be stressed is that, what-ever was gained by the triumph of 'clarity', logic and Descartes, the gain was paid for by an immeasurable loss...you can't subscribe to assump-tions implicit in 'clear and 'logical' as criteria without cutting yourself off from most important capacities and potentialities of thought which of its nature is essentially heuristic and creative" (Ortolano, 2005: 16).

Clearly there have been massive advances following the Enlightenment and industrial revolutions for the developments of states and societies in creating wealth, living standards, life expectancy and culture for example. However, the twentieth and twenty-first centuries, with their two world wars, the Holocaust and genocides, the use of nuclear weapons, the threat of nuclear annihilation, global warming, pollution, massive inequality, entrenched poverty, etc.demonstrates that progress is not unlimited and comes at a price. For both Leavis and Bohm we are sleep walking away from creativity and into an abyss of our own making. The need for acts of consciousness and the provision of an alternate vision is one that has to move us beyond the closed world of mimetic currency values where repeated endorsement confirms the status of self-evident truths (see Collini, 2013) (books, literature or academic papers are valued on the basis of their best seller, top of the charts, or most cited status). In busy lives we all want and need reductive instrumentalism (maybe it is as Erich Fromm (2001) says a fear of freedom) and prefer (as Allan Bloom argues (1987)) to read summaries and books about books rather than the original books themselves. It is interesting talking to publishers of academic texts who increasingly argue for those texts to be "accessible" and in "plain English". The same is happening on university campus' and the processes of designing degree programmes. The presumption is that the reader/student should not have to engage with and do too much work with the text, and thus their own thought. This fragmentation and loss of thought leads to a loss of mind/soul, and the ability to find a collective language to challenge the failures of modernity. A loss of coherent thought structure can be found in aspects of post modernity and its emphasis on hyper individualism and permanent insecurity (see Hall & Winlow, 2015). If Descartes provides the structure of body, soul, mind and matter, then Kant does the same for agency where freedom is the realm where the subject establishes his own limit and so limits are intrinsic rather than imposed (de Castro Rocha, 2019). This limit is limited further by any communication of the self, being a process of reduction, or rather in giving form to the content of communication we seek to apply judiciously Ockham's razor. In this way, we can remove the superfluous to say clearly, what we have to say and to assert our positions, *res cogitans*. To put this another way Descartes' "I think therefore I am" becomes "I think reductively therefore I am reduced".

In addressing these issues, the development of Girard's thought in respect of the two cultures can be marked by two key symposiums that he organised, and which also reveal the richness and power of his approach in reaching across disciplines to research and explain culture and the importance of science. Firstly, a symposium at Johns Hopkins university in 1966 entitled "The Language of Criticism and the Sciences of Man", secondly at Stanford University in 1981 a symposium on "Order and Disorder". The first launched the careers of Barthes, Hyppolite, Derrida, and Lacan in the USA. Michel Foucault, having said that he would attend, was "notoriously absent" (Schullenberger, 2021) and maybe if he had attended, then given their shared interests in violence and institutions then there may have been some rich developments in criminological theory, we will never know. As it was the *avant-garde* of French thought at the height of structuralism went on to become household name intellectuals with rock star status; the same is not true for Girard. As Haven (2018: 122) states,

> René Girard would champion a system of thought that was both a child of this new era and an orphan within it. He was at once proud of his role in launching the symposium and troubled by some of its consequences.

The Hopkins' symposium (published by Macksey & Donato, 1972) was intended to mark the crowning achievements of structuralism (so much so that Claude Lévi-Strauss, unable to attend, had nonetheless given the event his blessing) but would seamlessly developed into post-structuralism; it was a seismic event. Girard himself saw that much of post-structuralist thought was itself vulnerable to mimetic contagion, and he soon became a detractor of "French theory" (Shullenberger, 2021). He understood the need for conceptualisation and theory building but argued that philosophers tended to get lost in concepts and ideas, at the expense of the empirical. But further, he had a problem with philosophical ethics, arguing that all moral philosophies are a legacy of the archaic sacrificial (scapegoat mechanism), and that ultimately truth expressed in religion and science converge and this common truth cannot be apprehended by moral philosophy (Dumouchel & Wilmes, 2017). I will address this argument in some detail as a key part of departure between the thinking of Athens and Jerusalem.

The Stanford Symposium was a coming together of the "two cultures" of science and the humanities including the Nobel Laureate for chemistry Ilya Prigogine and Elizabeth Stengers in examining the relationship between order and disorder in the natural world (see Livingstone, 1981).

This marks a maturing of Girard's thought in understanding developments in positivism and how this relates to the rich qualitative and diverse aspects of cultural life and their non-reducibility, and marks a significant overlap with the study of non-linearity through chaos and complexity theory (see Pycroft & Bartollas, 2014). In this paradigm, the victim status becomes a cultural attractor, a "magnetic field" which sets up highly predictable patterns. In Chaos theory "chaos" is the natural output of highly deterministic systems, and so are not chaotic at all in the ordinary sense of the word. Girard would argue that in the systems that we call societies and cultures, there is a sensitivity to the initial conditions that we call the victimage mechanism. If the ongoing health crises in the developed world are due to an overwhelming of our genetic makeups which are still programmed for living on the African savannah, then this is true, also for our failures to grasp non-violence. The dove of peace always appears as a mythical return to mechanical solidarity and escaping the uncertainty of the modern world and its organic solidarity. Organic solidary is precarious and uncertain and so does not feel like solidarity at all but rather permanent crisis. This crisis is further deepened by the "deep magic[1]" of scapegoating no longer working (its outcomes are at best short term and therefore sub-optimal). An exploration of Durkheim is fruitful in revealing these dynamics but also functionalism as a forerunner of systems theory enables a detailed understanding of the causal mechanisms (often obscured in cultural and institutional practices) that act as feedback loops to maintain a system of violence that is in equilibrium. This approach to complexity theory understands the ways in which information is processed through networks and is contained at every point in the whole system e.g. why and how does the rampaging mob which is terrorising immigrants have unanimity of purpose? There is significant overlap here not just with complexity theory but also Dragan Milovanovic's (2014) Quantum Holographic Criminology, itself an audacious and inspiring attempt to overcome the twos cultures divide. I will explore those relationships and offer a development of Milovanovic's work through an application of the de Broglie-Bohm version of quantum

---

[1] The language of the deep and deeper magic from the dawn of time will be familiar to readers of C.S Lewis Narnia stories. He was a leading protestant Christian commentator in the 20th Century and his books are themselves a re-mythologisation of Christianity within a Greek context. Particularly he advocates penal substitution theory which arises from Anselm onwards (see below) itself a retelling of the sacred sacrificial.

mechanics, linked to the idea of *haecceitas*. This approach enables an understanding of desire as the key to societal development based upon consciousness of self, realised in the other. The self is already whole and in flowing movement creatively expressing desire and yet experiences fragmentation in the face of perceived threat of adversity.

CHAPTER 3

Learning to See

Abstract This section will explore the ways in which we learn to see and understand our own desires, and the ways in which those desires are mimetic rather than authentic, thus leading to scapegoating and violence. The role of Judaeo-Christianity in exposing the truths of these dynamics are explored in the light of Nietzsche and the critical tradition in philosophy and criminology.

Keywords Gospel narratives · *Méconnaissance* · Nietzsche · Postmodern · Unconscious · Unconcealment · Difference · Will to power · Will to power of Christianity · Death of God · Ontotheology · Administrative victimology · Mastery over nature · New rationality

The gospel narratives are the foundation for a profound level of disruption and change in human society grounded in love and non-violence. A clue to the advantages of Girard's work are encapsulated in Dupuy's quip about psychoanalysis in that this system introduces a personal dimension, a challenge to us all, to understand and change our complicity in the inter-individual violence that is common to all social settings including the criminal justice system. Learning to see and lift the veil of what Girard calls *méconnaissance* (Fr. Things misconstrued, misrecognised) does not require lengthy and expensive psychoanalysis, rather the gospel of love

A. Pycroft, *René Girard and Criminal Justice*, Palgrave Pioneers in Criminology, https://doi.org/10.1007/978-3-031-82471-5_3

and forgiveness in its radical equality is open to each and every one of us. In this respect, Girardian thought presents us with a model that points us towards truth, but is itself not truth, and it is worth bearing in mind his own words in discussing Nietzsche,

"The piety of Nietzsche's disciples – the sanctimonious and blind piety that surrounds only dead models, of course in our Nietzschean world, prevents the truth from being heard or even uttered." (Girard, 1976: 1258)

The Girardian model enables me to examine what it means to be a practitioner within the criminal justice system and how I can make sense of myself and the decisions that I make within the context of institutional justice and the impacts those decisions have on criminals, victims and communities. Practitioners are now micro technicians of risk management whose practices are obscured and elevated by the ontotheological ethics of punishment often masquerading as rehabilitation (Pycroft, 2021). In turn the postmodern turn in critical criminology reads like a long list of sectional interests, Black, Queer, Feminist, Convict, etc. all competing with each other for attention and the allocation of scarce resources, bereft of a language by which to communicate. Paradoxically, despite a powerful critique emerging from de-centring the subject the only communication is through the metaphysical battleground of the law itself (law and the practices of justice function as sacred sacrificial religion in everything but name) and usually the demand for harsher sentences for particular kinds of crimes relevant to those groups. Thus, these theories are limited in what they can offer the practitioner in addressing their responsibilities to the common good, given there is no agreement on what the common good actually, might or ought to be.

Girard's argument that the Judaeo-Christian scriptures reveal the sacrificial victim mechanism that is at the heart of all human culture has been highly influential across a range of disciplines, but not criminology. This despite Girard's being a radical victimology that literally deifies the victim and helps us to understand our own unconscious complicity in violence. To some degree, it would appear that these unconscious drives negate the possibility of escaping violence, and thus Girard's worldview is apocalyptic. Therefore, while Girard's thought has been utilised as a hermeneutic of suspicion in the humanities and social science, within those disciplines little attention is paid to the solutions to these problems that he suggests. That is because he argues for a personalist ethics grounded in *imitatio Dei* (see Jun, 2007). Not only does this approach appear to challenge the very foundations of liberal democracy, its claims to rationality and separation from myth, but it also undermines the claims of dominant scholastic theology with respect to atonement (see later) and its justifications for retributive practices. The question is which God we want to imitate, and whether we want to imitate the Judaeo- Christian God, who is angry, vengeful and demanding of retribution and for that reason cannot be a resource in restorative justice (See Johnstone & Ness, 2007), or a God of love and forgiveness. The apparent complexity of this choice is demonstrated by the fact that restorative justice is just as confused about the meaning of forgiveness and how to work with it as everyone else (see e.g. Armour & Umbreit, 2005). In truth the more that processes of restorative justice are assimilated into normative and statu-tory structures of justice then the less likely it will be for forgiveness to be addressed. It was observed by Hal Pepinskey (2006) that when you have alternatives to punishment, the punishments themselves become harsher. We can observe this in the UK with the probation service, a theological enterprise set up as an alternative to punishment. Following the punitive turn, this became punishment in the community and any discussions of an increased use of community sentences to address prison overcrowding are always predicated on those sentences being as tough as prison sentences. This is a clear example of an escalation to extremes. To help us to make sense of both our cultural and universal slavery to punishment rather than exploring approaches to forgiveness Girard reveals much of what the Christian narrative obscures. In the words of Richard Kearney (1999: 252):

Girard seeks accordingly to make the operations of our social imaginary – i.e. our ideological unconscious – answerable to ethics. He resolves to subject ideologies of scapegoating to critical hermeneutics of suspicion, exposing concealed meanings behind apparent ones ... sacrificial figures though invariably aliens and excoriated by their contemporaries become hallowed over the ages until they are eventually remembered as saviour gods who restored their community from chaos to order. They emerge out of the mists of time as miraculous 'others' who managed to transmute conflict into law. But this miraculous alteration of sacrificed 'aliens' into sacred 'others' is predicated upon a strategic forgetfulness of their original stigmatisation.

In guiding this task of hermeneutics, it appears on first sight that this unconcealment is the same as the Delphic maxim to "know thyself". However, I want to explore the differences between the Greek concepts of pharmakós and Jewish practices of atonement. Pharmakós is the *deus ex machina* solution whereby we create out Gods through the scapegoat mechanism and we become metaphysically enslaved, it is a self-fulfilling prophecy. Expressed thus by Girard "Myth is the guilt of Oedipus; Truth is the innocence of Christ" (1994: cited in Heim (2006): 37), whereby Greek myth obscures violence and so even Oedipus is an innocent victim of a scapegoating mechanism and the play should be read as a text of persecution. The trial and execution of Jesus is the complete opposite where for the first time in history the victim of the mob is revealed to be innocent and so fundamentally shifts our perspective and work history.

The texts that became the Christian New Testament were of course translated into Greek but we need to beware of ancient Greeks bearing gifts of insight. If as Bertrand Russell is correct that that all Western philosophy is a footnote to Plato, then that philosophy is a footnote to pharmakós. Girard understood this and is why he distanced himself from philosophy and became increasingly interested in theology. In essence, Greek thought and its influence and re-emergence in key points in history as an expression of the violent sacred sacrificial is at best a problematic resource for an understanding of self in the light of the other. Girard's great insight is that while we can always recognise people who are being scapegoated, we can never see our own acts of scapegoating as we feel completely justified in our approach (2003). As with Emmanuel Levinas Girard prioritises alterity over ontology (see Doran, 2017) expressed by Levinas as "first ethics" and Girard that "all desire is a desire for being" (cited in Haven (2023: vii). This knowing of self, and understanding of self within the contextual relationships of organisation and society, and the meaning of rationality is the heart of the crisis that is criminal justice. The question that is fundamental to all relationships and understanding acts of personal and institutional discrimination is "am I scapegoating?" In answering, I need to subject myself to a hermeneutic of suspicion. Such an approach is a commitment to equality with the other and is the antithesis of the romantic tradition that all desires, including those for retribution are authentic. In addressing the origin of my desires that appear as foundational to social order the criminal justice apocalypse (the punitive turn in justice and its consequences) can either be a source of revelation and change for myself and others through a hermeneutic of affirmation or a continued nihilist descent into escalating violence. In a world of post-modern fluidity, we have lost the understanding that the violence both committed by criminals and done to them in justified response to that crime is real, not only because we label it as such. The crisis of the criminal justice system is a metaphysical crisis of meaning with the language of rehabilitation obscuring the day-to-day violence experienced by those on remand and those convicted of offences, and the language of victim rights obscuring the violence done to those demanding satisfaction for the wrong done to them. Both offer a teleological promise that is deceitful and no better than "jam tomorrow".

Girard returns us to an exploration of the Judaeo-Christian tradition and what he finds there is the dynamic nature of reality, but not as expressed in the logos of Heraclitus (*Pólemos*—the divine embodiment of war) with a consequent Nietzschean will to power perpetuating violence (the eternal recurrence of the same) but rather the truth of the Johannine logos (see Prologue to John's Gospel Chapter 1 v 1–18) as the divine embodiment of God *non cupidi vindictae* (not desirous of vengeance). Thus, rather than articulating a re-mythologisation through Greek tragedy and revenge apropos Nietzsche (the great philosopher of revenge), there is a revelation and affirmation of a ground of being that is generatively non-violent but needing the right conditions for "good" mimesis to flourish. Good mimesis is not simply modelling "pro social" behaviours but a range of gifts that are always a supplement that counter the violence of Greek thought predicated as it is on *pharmakós* and exclusionary practices. Girard (see Adams &Girard, 1993), and also Derrida (1968) agree that the supplement is added from the outside as a gift. This gift is a gift of grace (see also Rieff, 2007) and is understood as supplying that which is missing. This unconditional gifting and act of hospitality when accepted thus appears to be already inscribed within that to which it is added; I have given you what is mine to give and it is yours. For example, the role of the good therapist, social worker or probation officer is to enable individuals to assume responsibility for their lives and are at best supplemental in that process, through the gifts they bring to the point where they are no longer required. When this happens, it is almost as if they had never been required. I remember working with street drinkers who would say to me that without them I would not have a job, to which my response was that I lived in the hope of redundancy. It might be described as the strange death of the social worker.

What the thought of Nietzsche revealed to Girard (1986) was that in the argument that Christianity was nothing but a slave mentality, a form of revenge against the strong that there was a kernel of truth in what he argued. What Girard saw was that in the Judaeo-Christian tradition, uniquely, the collected mythos were written from the perspective of the innocent victim who had been religiously sacrificed (scapegoated) to resolve some kind of crisis. For Girard myth always contains an element of truth that reveals that real people have experienced real violence that is forgotten in the creation of those myths but not completely erased. The fullness of Girard's perspective also provides us then with a survivor-ology through stories of lived experiences of resistance, redemption and healing by the victim. In particular, Girard's approach helps us to apprehend the ways in which our own complicity in expressing universal concern for those who we perceive as genuinely innocent victims both leads to demands for retribution, and a desire for "rehabilitation". Who the victim is, is the key question. The problem for 20th Century approaches to rehabilitation were that the criminal was seen as the real victim of society's failures and forgot the victim of the actual crime to whom harm had been done, or worse questioned whether it was crime at all. This led to a crisis of differentiation and ultimately the punitive turn to reinstate the difference between the innocent victim and the guilty criminal. A great service was done by Left Realism in empirically rediscovering the victim of crime, but all of this reinforces Richard Quinney's (1995) argument that our primary concern should be a contextual approach to social justice rather than a reductionist focus on criminal acts. This social justice needs a clearly articulated ontology and epistemology underpinning the hard work of mending broken and dysfunctional relationships. Neither victim, nor criminal nor community need to be expelled by the other.

In criminal justice, Nils Christie (1977) identifies this problem of undifferentiation in his conflicts as property argument. Christie (1977: 1) argues that his "suspicion is that criminology to some extent has amplified a process where conflicts have been taken away from the parties directly involved and thereby have either disappeared or become other people's property. In both cases a deplorable outcome". Christie argues for the importance of individuals owning their conflicts as a source of creativity rather than having them stolen by the depersonalising forces of the state in the form of lawyers and treatment professionals. This depersonalisation is another form of fragmentation and disjunction designed to resolve conflict in the name of a greater good by those professionals. With regard to treatment personnel, he argues that their function is to convert "the image of the case from one of conflict into one of non- conflict" (Christie, 1977: 4), with the non-conflict perspective being a precondition for defining crime as a legitimate target for treatment. In both the legal and treatment settings there is increased specialisation, bureaucratisation and hence the development of trained incapacity. Building upon the work of Thorstein Veblen, the philosopher Kenneth Burke (Burke, 1954) developed the concept of trained incapacity, which refers to situations whereby one's abilities actually function as blindness. Burke (1954: 7) gives the example of businesspeople "[w] ho through long training in competitive finance, have so built their scheme of orientation about this kind of effort and ambition that they cannot see serious possibilities in any other system of production and distribution".

Both state and religious law is violence, a combination of both is lethal and uncontrolled. This was understood by Jesus of Nazareth who also understood that those who resort to the law cannot be satisfied, or those who receive punishment be transformed. Those who do not right their wrongs before being taken to court may well experience violence as a consequence. Robert Cover, (1995) observes,

> "Legal interpretation takes place in a field of pain and death...Legal interpretive acts signal and occasion the imposition of violence upon others: A judge articulates her understanding of a text, and as a result, somebody loses his freedom, his property, his children, even his life. Interpretations in law also constitute justifications of violence which has already occurred or is about to occur. When interpreters have finished their work, they frequently leave behind victims whose lives have been torn apart by these organized, social practices of violence. Neither legal interpretation nor the violence it occasions may be properly understood apart from one another."

If Vattimo and Girard's (2006) assertion is correct that strong institutions require strong ontological justifications then this would be particularly true for the practices of criminal justice as with the decline of church and monarchy it effectively becomes the last remaining religion. The sacred sacrificial provides just such metaphysically strong thoughts, theologically linked. Girard's work reinforces the argument about legal punishment as civil religion, namely that with the decline of church the criminal justice system which has grown out of religious practices operates in the same way but with those origins obscured. The Jesus of forgiveness works with the weakness which the world[1] cannot (and refuses to) comprehend, as it is perceived as death to the self in the evolutionary drive to survive. Girard's work has revived a two cities thesis of history in the Augustinian tradition (see Milbank, 2006) and in proclaiming the truth gospels (underpinned by rationality and empiricism, he is in the positivist tradition, contra nihilism or realism) provides us with a necessary sacrificial reading of the foundations of criminology and victimology as academic disciplines which through their state-sponsored functions have both obscured and enabled the continuation of the sacred sacrificial in the form of state violence underpinned and justified by claims on Christian theology. A consequence of this return to the archaic sacrificial in the development of the modern state and its institutions of justice founded on atonement theory (see below) is an acceptance that the violent apocalyptic comes from God and not humanity. Therefore, I can punish the other with impunity and with impeccable metaphysical credentials and justifications. There is a need to differentiate here the violence of God and the violence of Man, the former does not exist, the latter imbues every aspect of our lives. The apocalyptic as revelatory of God's love in our lived experience is more akin to epiphany which cannot be enforced. In our apparently secular, postmodern and post-truth orientated world, this marginal interest in religion as a problem rather than a solution obscures the foundational truth of violence at the heart of our institutions.

In Europe the role of the Christian church has been pivotal in shaping the nature of nation states but also the dispensation of justice, its understanding and justification. There is no question that the series of reformations that occurred in the Western church from the twelfth century onwards, leading to increased centralisation and reduced collegiality through a strong Papacy coincided with the development of what we now identify as the modern state and requiring a strong

---

[1] In Judaism and early Christianity, Satan, rather than having a being, is, through accusation (French: j'accuse), hindrance or temptation, the illusory obstacle to *tikkun olam* (Hebrew: repairing the world) and the overcoming of idolatry (https:// www. jewish virtual library.org/ satan). Also, Stokes (2014) shows from the biblical evidence that the noun śātān (transliteration from the Hebrew) relates specifically to physical attack. In this sense, another person can be my śātān or I can be a śātān to another person. The scapegoating mechanism, and the metaphysical and collective violence of all against the one, to resolve communal crises is in this sense, and the sense in which Jesus identified it, is satanic.

ontology. Particularly in the scholastic period from Anselm of Canterbury onwards (11th Century) and the development of universities both law and theology as academic and rational disciplines drew off each other for metaphysical justification (see Gorringe, 1996). It would appear that (as Gorringe, (1996) argues) that the satisfaction theory of atonement was a central part of the development of crime and punishment.

The Christian Churches' own historical will to power and the implications for criminal justice are outlined by Gorringe (1996) and Pycroft and Bartollas (2018) focussing on arguments for the nature of atonement and the necessity of the death of Jesus to satisfy the demands of an angry and demanding God (satisfaction theory).In his magisterial work on religion and the decline of magic, Keith Thomas (1978) makes the point that while at the local level priests and religious would collude with superstitious practices, nonetheless the teaching authority of the church was based on the rational exploration and explanation of not just revelation but the world in which we live. Likewise, Paul Friedland (2014) argues contra Foucault (1977) that spectacular punishments in mediaeval France were actually a public liturgy that secured social cohesion rather than the public being repressed and deterred by those punishments. Nonetheless (as Friedland argues) those who committed murder were required to recompense the victim's family and also make amends to God. This scholastic view of natural law which developed from Anselm and Aquinas whereby every sin and crime had to be punished was influenced by the "rediscovery" of Greek thought via the Islamic scholars Ibn Sīnā (Latinised to Avicenna) and Ibn Rushd (Latinised to Averroes). The medieval scholastic Christian philosophers were indebted to them for their translations of Aristotle. The philosophy of Aristotle and its elitist purity may have provided a rational framework for interpreting theology, but its consequences were to make the love of God and neighbour conditional with the effect of reintroducing and justifying the necessity of punishment linked to the sacred sacrificial. As Gorringe argues "the gift of grace expressed in the Pauline letters, and the cross of Christ is not a justification of punishment but a heralding of its end" (1996: 269).

If Girard's argument is correct that the execution of Jesus was intended to herald the end of the violent sacrificial then the Holocaust was the denouement of 2000 years of Christian history that had in some respects engaged in its own will to power through scapegoating the Jews. Within these complex processes there was initially a crisis of differentiation between the early Jewish sect that became Christianity and the Jewish religion who did not accept Jesus as the Messiah. Arguments over whether Jesus forgave the Jews ("Forgive them Father, as they know not what they do") as he was dying which have persisted over the centuries simply indicate the power of the sacred sacrificial and a rejection of the power of love and forgiveness. It is this form of Christianity that is appropriated by the medieval nascent nation state in a collaborative will to power that continues to underpin our approach to criminal justice, punishment and rehabilitation (see Gorringe, 1996).

For Marion (2012), God is beyond being and is absolutely free in all determinations and the failure of metaphysics is precisely to ascribe categories of being to Him. He argues that Nietzsche not only reveals the death of the metaphysical God, but under her various conceptual names metaphysical idols are imposed on a God who has yet to be encountered. Marion is then arguing for the death of a certain kind of God, namely the God of punishment who has become the idol of the criminal justice system in all its justifications. Marion, then calls God by the most theological of names "Charity" with the revelation of agape within it and in his thought being removed from aspects of human destiny, belonging neither to pre-, post- nor modernity. This is the irruption of grace (e.g. Paul does not talk about forgiveness, but rather the gift of grace to undeserving people—see Bash, 2015) and is what I take to be affirmation and to be found in the totality of the situation (see Pycroft & Bartollas, 2022). This affirmation is: ...made actual for each of us precisely in the totality of the situation—material, psychological, moral and spiritual combined—in which we find ourselves at each single moment of our conscious life (Butler, 1981) This is also what Michael DeValve (2015) calls a love and healing that transforms rather than is controlling and having power over others. It is a love that never ceases giving and enables the challenging of the power/fear paradigm. This position is weak and always marginal relying on ground up and local initiatives that cannot be created by top down control mechanisms. In this context, the individual becomes an agent of change connected to their wider context (change is ex materia rather than ex nihilo) and open to possibilities of being that do not require that the other becomes the model (competitor) for my desires.

At the heart of this argument is the difference between aseity and ab alio. In the Christian doctrine of the Holy Trinity (Father, Son and Holy Spirit) each is the model for the other and where there is no competition and rivalry, giving entirely of the self to the other without loss of identity, meaning or purpose. Identity, meaning and purpose are endlessly created anew. It is only through acknowledging the necessity of the existence of a God without being, that we do not create her in our own image by ascribing metaphysical characteristics and Marion (2012) argues that God needs to be released from this ontotheology. A consequence of this metaphysic following Anselm through Aquinas is that in responding to evil then revenge is seen as the only remedy, with: The height of evil (consisting) in perpetuating evil with the intent of suppressing suffering, in rendering others guilty in order to guarantee one's own innocence. For the more I want to assure my innocence—as is quite natural!—the more I discharge my sufferings and my responsibilities on someone else, in short, the more I engulf him in evil (Marion, 2002:8).

However, Girard enables us to see that secularism itself is the child of Christianity but which (as Nietzsche understood) still contains traces of the archaic religious and sacred sacrificial that Christianity has deconstructed.

> "God is dead. God remains dead. And we have killed him. How shall we comfort ourselves, the murderers of all murderers? What was holiest and mightiest of all that the world has yet owned has bled to death under our knives: who will wipe this blood off us? What water is there for us to clean ourselves? What festivals of atonement, what sacred games shall we have to invent? Is not the greatness of this deed too great for us? Must we ourselves not become gods simply to appear worthy of it?" (Nietzsche, 1974: 111)

In the criminal justice system, the traces are particularly thick as a repository of the scapegoating mechanism that we can cohere around and communicate over for the creation of social order. Forgiveness is the hermeneutic key that un-conceals the collapsing temple of punishment but which brings the unbearable and unwelcome weight of responsibility. We can no long opt out through capital punishment[2] and asking that "God have mercy on your soul", or permanently exclude and "thrown away the key": the gospel is the gospel of peace, a peace which can only come from a God who enables us to embrace equality through assuming

---

[2] In 1215 the Lateran Council of the Western Church both outlawed trials by ordeal thus bringing in trial by jury, and also forbade priests from blessing capital punishments and now could only minister to the condemned. I assume that this is the origins of chaplaincy.

responsibility and love. If the scapegoat mechanism is foundational to society based on the aleatory victim then systems of justice, reduce the risk of it being me who is scapegoated. In a rational society, we can dispense with mercy which is associated with monarchy and hierarchy contra equality (see Bull, 2019) and direct with even more ire our feelings of outrage and engage in liturgically re-enacting the crime (see Friedland, 2014) however, we no longer accept that a resolution is possible for serious crimes. A retreat from the death penalty means the need for a new language of inclusion. If the scapegoat had prevented societies falling back into destructive rivalries of all against all with law and justice becoming the repetition of the sacred sacrificial masked by the veil of rationality, then the limit of that rationality is revealed. In the absence of a cadaver around which we all cohere, then we are apparently helpless and lost.

The restoration of peace through forgiveness is a visible restoration of equality that has been transgressed through rivalry and domination. Victimology has become administrative in the service of the state, and uses the concept of the innocent victim as a metaphysically Christian status to justify harsh punishments. Girard (2001: 178) argues,

> "The current process of spiritual demagoguery and rhetorical overkill has transformed the concern for victims into a totalitarian command and permanent inquisition. The media themselves notice this and make fun of "victimology" which doesn't keep them from exploiting it. The fact that our world has become solidly anti-Christian, at least among its elites, does not prevent the concern for victims from flourishing – just the opposite. The majestic inauguration of the "post-Christian era" is a joke. We are living through a caricatural "ultra-Christianity" that tries to escape from the Judeo-Christian orbit by "radicalizing" the concern for victims in an anti-Christian manner

As James Alison (2003) has argued, where Nietzsche and Girard meet then theology is forged, and I argue that this meeting place becomes a possibility for informing both a critical criminology and also a language for change. This approach also helps us to understand why despite the crises in the criminal justice systems in the UK and USA there is little desire or ability for change. The criminological imagination has shrunk into reductionism whether expressed as narrow decontextualised positivism or postmodern subjectivity. In seeking new ethical frameworks whether or how to act is the key normative question when faced with the risk of being assimilated as passive automata within a bureaucratic criminal justice system or in seeking a new language of collective creativity. At some point we have to stop playing bourgeois academic language games and actually engage with the other and ethically there are always opportunities, challenges and choices open to every practitioner. In Girardian terms this is a learning to see my own complicity in the violence that maintains social order and as Eagleton (2003) argues this insight returns us to the big questions of truth, virtue, objectivity and morality rejected by postmodern social theory. Girard enables us to tell the big story of criminal justice and it is this narrative that has to be the concern of practitioners too, and regarding of themselves and their actions and their place in that story. In reviewing the work of Girard as "cultural criminology" Malcolm Bull (*nd*) lists what he sees as the embarrassing crimes of Girard against academic convention including being; explicitly didactic, unashamedly anachronistic, impenitently ethnocentric; but nonetheless concludes that Girard does provide a unique vantage point from which to review our own assumptions and that the source of this embarrassment may be due to self-consciousness. It is this challenging of assumptions starting with myself and questioning my own authenticity that is central to being able to effectively help people and bring about societal change. However, the key Girardian argument is that I understand myself in the light of the other, as the other is the source of my desires. All desire is a desire for being and I want to be the other, which brings me into conflict with the model of my desire thus leading to contagious violence. As Ernst Cassirer (1967) argues we need a new instrument of thought and an examination of what we mean by rationality; in the modern context instrumental rationality is expressed as bureaucratic power. It is this utilitarian power that behind its transactions conceals the violence done to all stakeholders in the criminal justice system and needs to be rethought (see Christie, 1977).

I argue that Girard provides us with a new instrument to examine that rationality in the light of what is conscious and unconscious, and is an approach that is above all concerned with learning to see what is really there. Following Husserl (2017) and in phenomenological terms that which we apprehend is given to us, and following Ricouer (2004) and in hermeneutical terms the apprehension of that gift can be a source of revelation. We need theory to help us to see what is real (in a positivist sense) and given Girard's concerns with the origins of violence, religion, institutions and representation you would think that this would be a mainstay of criminological thought if only as a source of dispute or point of departure. In my view, the question of this exclusion or oversight, or simple non-recognition of his work, goes to the heart of criminology both as a project of modernity in the sense of mastery over human nature, the capacity to change it, as well as the existential and post-modern revolts against the technological tyranny that has followed from those projects. But what Girardian thought effectively does is to decon-struct criminology both as a project of modernity, through revealing criminal justice as a bastion of the sacred sacrificial, but also the fail-ures of postmodern thought to address those problems. A reification of *la différence* neither gives us a language by which to communicate or enables the conditions for a new language to emerge. Our understanding of social order in Western Europe has emerged from between Athens and Jerusalem, mediated by Roman Law, not least through Christian doctrines of atonement (from the 10th Century onwards), underpinning criminal justice. If as Girard argues the shadow of the sacred sacrificial looms large in contemporary institutions of justice, then then this raises the important question of where new resources can emerge from, and whether truth events can happen *ex nihilo* (see e.g. Badiou, 2003). In developing Girardian thought, I will be arguing that forgiveness, anthro-pologically grounded in Judaeo-Christianity demonstrates the emergence of a new rationality and the radically new. This rationality is premised on the demythologising of culture, the revelation of violence therein, and the imperative to engage in love as the new verb for being.[3]

Girard and Eagleton agree that the age of social theory that followed from Nietzsche's deconstruction is over with Eagleton (2003) arguing that politics and ethics are in fact inextricably linked,

> Radical politics is a re-education of our desires...you...can...be mistaken about whether you are flourishing, and someone else may be more widely perceptive about the matter than yourself. This is one important sense in which morality is objective (p.129)

It was Eagleton (2003) in reflecting on the demise of cultural theory who said "at just the point that we have begun to think small, history

---

[3] In criminology Michael DeValve (2015) has been a prophetic voice in the wilderness in talking about love. I am indebted to him for his friendship and support and enabling me to follow his lead.

has begun to act big", with reference to the events of 9/11, the War on Terror, the return of religion in the form of Islam. Hollowed out by both positivism and a narrow reductionism which reduces culture to a reproductive and material instrumentalism, we have become small and social theory cannot find a way out of our violence, based as it is on the "romantic lie" of Rousseau that people are fundamentally good and thus all desires are authentic. We need to talk in bald terms about the big picture which we no longer see, or do not want to paint for fear of harming the other. Unfortunately, this postmodern individualism and fear of engaging the other has seen the continuation of the sacred sacrificial and in Orwellian double think we can e.g. end up with prisons claiming that they are engaging in trauma informed care, or where compulsory and coerced therapeutic treatments are delivered where the concerns of the state as a proxy for the victim are effectively the focus of the therapeutic work. The big picture of criminal justice is that it does not work in reducing crime because it is not intended to work, and it cannot work. This will be discussed further with respect to Robert Martinson and his death as the founding murder that reveals the truth of the criminal justice system.

Mastery over nature and including human nature since the seventeenth century has been predicated on the collective murder of God, but in having assumed mastery we have abdicated responsibility for the apocalyptic circumstances in which we find ourselves—environmental, nuclear, and poverty. We can include in this mass incarceration and mass community supervision and the myth of rehabilitation. To alleviate the crises, we scapegoat and sacrifice usually to the Gods whom we name as our ideologies leading to short term gain and long-term failure. Mimetic theory is inter-individual, it is political and as Jesus points out is foundational to social order and morality. The revelation of love and the renunciation of violence as the foundation of being enables us to be present to the other for their human flourishing and thus I achieve my own (see Eagleton, 2003: 138).

> Other persons are objectivity in action. It is exactly because they are fellow subjects that they can reveal to us their otherness and in that act disclose to us their own

Intersubjectivity and overcoming the Cartesian structure/agency divide are central to the questions that Girard raises and we now have resources on a number of fronts to address these questions which are being applied to criminology and to further his work. These resources in addressing the relationship between consciousness and matter in complexity theory and quantum mechanics (see Milovanovic, 2014; Pycroft, 2018; Pycroft & Bartollas, 2014, 2018, 2022) bring together the two cultures. In this developing work the use of postmodern philosophies has become important to address the dynamic, complex and fluid nature of reality and which seeks to address the ethics of human relationships with respect to crime, its context and aftermath but with competing visions of human flourishing. Unexpectedly, despite the death of God, religion has re-emerged as a key locus of enquiry and once again we find ourselves between Athens and Jerusalem. It is argued by Jean-Luc Marion (2012) that in examining the relationship between philosophical nihilism and the demanding openings of Christian revelation that at times the discourse comes together so closely that the antagonists appear to have a common course. I agree with this position and that a hermeneutic of suspicion reveals the failures of metaphysics, but in developing a hermeneutic of affirmation we need to go beyond Holy Saturday (which is as far as Slavoj Žižek will go in this thought (2011)) to Easter Sunday. We have the diagnosis, so how do we address the problem? Clearly the use of modern and rational perspectives to interpret religious myth requires a theology (Jerusalem, Mecca and Varanasi, etc.), and all cultures and societies have founding myths. In my own work, I have been working with theologians to develop research projects on forgiveness and religious literacy (the use of religious language for civic purposes) which is often a part of the problem as well as the solution (e.g. conflict and post conflict in Northern Ireland). This will always be marginal work, precisely because inter subjectivity is by its nature unpredictable; peace, love, healing and forgiveness are non-linear and will always frustrate "scientists" and do not win votes for politicians. However, I can talk about my own violence to you, and explain it through the language of Athens and Jerusalem, and I am open to listening to you about yours, whatever language or framework you want to use, and this might just be the beginning of a dialogue (perhaps we can invite others, including some non-criminologists too?). Is this not what peacemaking really is? (Girard, 2010: *ix*).

CHAPTER 4

The Relationship Between Myth, Reason and Mimetic Theory

Abstract This section will explore Girard's mimetic model and discusses its relationship to scapegoating, and how the reality of violence is concealed within myths from around the world, providing and anthropological context for Girard's work.

Keywords Anthropology · Frazer · Scapegoat · Intersubjectivity · Alterity · Ontology

All communication is a form of reduction, namely something is always lost in the telling, writing and singing. However, in seeking to overcome the reductionism inherent in most forms of communication to enable an embracing of the complex nature of reality then the writer, artist, poet, musician or dancer has an advantage in communicating acts of consciousness. The art of communication is in what the other apprehends, with the necessity for a certain degree of congruence between the communicator and those they communicate to (transference, intuition and empathy) and vice versa. With Leavis, we can look to poesis to provide a human muse that enables a more expansive thought concerning what I take to be our shared (if not sole) interest, namely the purpose and application of criminology to real people and real situations. Poesis, is neglected in criminology in comparison to natural philosophy or ethics but nonetheless allows for the emergence of this paper, the thinking of the thought the written of the writing, the reading of the read. The thingness of this thing is its haecceity. We are conscious in the world rather than of it (see Pycroft, 2018) and hermeneutical phenomenology unlocks the relationship between myth (histories of collective consciousness) and reason. The inability to apprehend the thing in itself is one of Kant's implicit limits, giving rise to liberalism, la difference and ultimately postmodernist post-truth, and the "alternative facts" of Donald Trump and Boris Johnson. Here Crewe is absolutely correct in seeing a corrective in the non-totalising philosophy of Levinas, in that we always have to consider the relationships between part and the whole (see Pycroft & Bartollas, 2014) and the necessity of the quality of my relationship with the other, whereby the other becomes the transcendent I. For Levinas, a process of kenosis (emptying of self) erases my ego for which I alone am responsible. This is the command that the other brings and an obligation that I cannot resist. However, events are real, and the risk of this approach is essentially the same as the new synthesis of Hegelian-Marxist dialectics, where events are forgotten in a new totalising whole (or hole, a black hole where all information if not destroyed is beyond the event horizon). With respect to transgression, calling to account (blame) and making good, there needs to be a confrontation with events, with the real, rather than the imaginary or the symbolic (in the Lacanian sense of these concepts). John Milbank (2006:395) argues that in the Judaeo-Christian tradition: Just as the act of creation takes nothing away from God, so also our self-giving involves no real self-loss, but it is rather a new reception of being, which consists fundamentally in orientation to the Other. It is this confrontation with events, expressed as history and what to do about it that is part of the crisis of the everyday in the criminal justice system. The writer and philosopher Jean Améry, a Jewish survivor of the Holocaust is very clear on this (1980) need to be heard and for a calling to account. But as Primo Levi (1986) recalls the unexpected ordinariness of the enemy you meet is disconcerting (I suppose this is what Hannah Arendt meant by the banality of evil (2006) and is challenging to make sense of (Arendt's work based on the trial of Adolph Eichman was highly criticised for seeing the horrors of the holocaust as banal). This, then is a problem of how I phenomenologically apprehend the other, within the context of personal history, as I always come between myself and that which I perceive/apprehend. Levinas sees this as a problem of solipsism and he is correct, but Girard's great insight (2003) is that the other becomes the model for my desire and thus a source of competition and escalation to violence. My own complicity in that violence is invisible to me, as my desire for what the other is based upon a blaming and holding to account of the other (as scapegoat) for which I feel fully justified. But the other's violence (and desire for what I have) is likewise invisible to themselves. A genuine intersubjectivity then has to accept complicity in violence to which we are all prone, and as Crewe (2019) indicates in quoting Richard Quinney (1991), this is at the heart of criminology as peacemaking. In this complicity we cannot apprehend Levinas' ethics as first philosophy, we are deaf, dumb and blind, to everything except our own desire reflected in the face of the other. The corrective to these realities is to be found in revisiting myth and interpreting those myths (including religious myth) in the light of modern scholarship (which is what restorative justice has sought to do, through looking to aboriginal sources for Justice). It is Nietzsche, the great philosopher of revenge who reboots myth now that God was dead. It would, however, be a mistake to think that Nietzsche's alternative myth does away with metaphysics and provides an ethic concerned with flesh and blood of the "here and now". The will to power of the *ubermensch* (the man who can reach over and above himself) sees Nietzsche soar to achieve nothing more than the instigation of a new metaphysical aristocracy, always at the expense of the *untermensch* (the term made infamous by the Nazis and which refers to the less than human).

In his psycho-analytically informed argument that scapegoating should not be seen as a conscious activity based on a conscious choice, Girard argues that the process is effective precisely because there is an element of delusion to which we are all susceptible. This means that all of us can condemn examples of scapegoating yet none of us can identify our own involvement in it. This is an example of what Girard identifies as méconnaissance which in the French can relate to a mistake, false information, illusion, misrecognition or mis-cognition, but for which there is no adequate and single definition in the English language. Girard (2003) argues that religion evolves precisely to contain violence in societies thus bringing about social order and culture (and is indebted to Durkheim, Freud and Frazer in this work). This is necessary because of the reality of mimetic rivalry which culminates in the war of all against all (and countering the "romantic lie" that people are essentially good), and an escalation to extremes.

"My hypothesis is mimetic: because humans imitate one another more than animals, they have had to find a means of dealing with contagious similarity, which could lead to the pure and simple disappearance of their society. The mechanism that reintroduces difference into a situation in which everyone has come to resemble everyone else is sacrifice. Humanity results from sacrifice; we are thus the children of religion. What I call after Freud the founding murder, in other words, the immolation of a sacrificial victim that is both guilty of disorder and able to restore order, is constantly re-enacted in the rituals at the origin of our institutions. Since the dawn of humanity, millions of innocent victims have been killed in this way in order to enable their fellow humans to live together, or at least not to destroy one another. This is the implacable logic of the sacred, which myths dissimulate less and less as humans become increasingly self-aware. The decisive point in this evolution is Christian revelation, a kind of divine expiation in which God through his Son could be seen as asking for forgiveness from humans for having revealed the mechanisms of their violence so late. Rituals had slowly educated them; from then on, humans had to do without." (Girard, 2010: ix)

The mimetic mechanism is a generative process (see, for example, Girard, 1987, 2003, 2007), the evidence for which can be found in myths of all kinds from around the world, but is particularly revealed in the Judaeo-Christian mythos. It covers a process that begins with mimetic desire, leading to mimetic rivalry, escalating to mimetic conflict and ends with the scapegoat resolution. Girard differentiates between desire and appetites with basic needs for biological survival not connected with desire. The latter is mimetic (imitative) and brought about by the presence of a model which is the key to his whole theory. Through mimesis, the subject will desire the same object possessed or desired by that model. The consequences of that desire are largely determined by proximity to that model, for example, I want what my celebrity hero has but we live in very different worlds and so a direct conflict between the two of us is not very likely as the objects of my model are beyond my reach. This is an externally mediated relationship. However, if my model is someone in my domain then their objects are accessible to me and this mimetic relationship is powerfully reinforcing (internally mediated) as both people imitate each other and become symmetrical doubles with an intense rivalry. The focus becomes the defeat of the other rather than the object itself, with the doubles becoming identical and undifferentiated: "A mimetic crisis is always a crisis of undifferentiation that erupts when the roles of subject and model are reduced to that of rivals. It's the disappearance of the object which makes it possible. This crisis not only escalates between the contenders, but it becomes contagious with bystanders" (Girard, 2007: 57).

Mimetic theory was a central concern for both Plato and Aristotle, but Girard develops and uses it in novel and innovative ways that fuse insights from evolutionary studies to develop a universal explanation for cultural formations, patterns and behaviours. Girard identifies mimesis as a law of social complexity that explains inter-individual relationships and the development of society. Girard by insisting on the revealed truth in Judaeo-Christianity the space of which is arrived at through empirical method directly challenges both enlightenment and postmodern thought.[1] Empirically Girard starts with Enlightenment view expressed by e.g. Frazer (1950) that religions as expressions of myth are all alike and through the accumulation of evidence argues that it is religion and sacrifice that develops to contain violence, and that uniquely it is Judaeo-Christianity that reveals the mechanisms therein.

Girard seeks to develop an interpretation of human culture based on genetics and evolution (Girard, 2007). His hypothesis, while relatively simple and apparently reductionist, acts in a generative capacity to drive the development of increasingly complex social and cultural phenomena. The evidence that Girard as literary theorist initially finds in the great writers is that humans are mimetic creatures and we desire what the other has. However, these desires become competitive until each becomes the other's rival with an escalation of violence involving a widening circle of people. This escalation has the potential to spiral out of control with the overpowering force of law being required to punish in a way that cannot be answered or resisted. Girard (1972) in asking how cultures managed to contain outbreaks of mimetic contagion (such as pogroms) without developed judicial systems (and we will return to the question of the crisis in modern justice) develops a theory of religion. As Johnsen (2019:31) argues,

---

[1] The granting of religious revelation its own integrity is not unusual in for example the phenomenological tradition (see Scheler), and phenomenology is the child of positivism.

"The great synthesizing but undertheorized movement in anthropology (Frazer, Freud and Durkheim) towards explaining the near universal dependence of archaic culture on religion and sacrifice challenged Girard to produce a better theory for religion than Frazer's version of scapegoating, Freud's version of the original victim or Durkheim's "effervescence" to produce instead a generative model which describes a non-deterministic mechanism to account for those effects, to explain the origin, survival and evolution of human culture in religion."

It is this secular literature that leads Girard to Christianity through understanding that it is religion that solves the problem of social violence, and is not the cause of that violence. Girard's argument is that human culture is sustained by the capability of religion to contain human violence through the evolution of sacrificial mechanisms in which the "war of all" can be resolved by focusing violence on one victim. This sacrificial scapegoat mechanism has miraculous powers because peace is established and social cohesion established. Controversially, Girard (2003) then argues that mimetic rivalry and the scapegoat mechanism as resolution is universally applicable to all cultures and is key to structuring those cultures, and for the participants there is always a degree of delusion involved. Hence all myths are based upon a lie that seeks to hide the violence committed, which is invariably an aleatory act committed against an innocent person, who is usually an outsider, someone with a physical or mental impairment.

CHAPTER 5

Deconstructing the Scapegoat: Sources of Non-violence Between Athens and Jerusalem

Abstract This section critically engages with Girard's conceptualisation of the scapegoat mechanism and the differences between ritual practices and understandings in Ancient Greece and Ancient Israel. It will be argued that seeing the distinction between these practices is essential in developing approaches to peacemaking.

Keywords Scapegoat · Day of Atonement · *Pharmakos* · Dionysus versus the Crucified

In times of crisis, a scapegoat (usually an outsider on the basis of gender, race, and ability) is randomly chosen to be excluded or killed. The sacrifice appears to resolve the crisis and period of peace commences, so much so that that the person sacrificed appears to have magical powers and is often deified. This victimage mechanism is institutionalised in religions. In the Judaeo-Christian tradition Leviticus 16 states that on the Day of Atonement, a number of sacrifices are required to make atonement by the High Priest. Firstly, he has to sacrifice a bull for his own sin and to make expiation for himself and his family. This is an explicit statement that the High Priest is not above the religious law and that he is complicit in sin and must be ritually purified before carrying out the actions on

A. Pycroft, *René Girard and Criminal Justice*, Palgrave Pioneers in Criminology, https://doi.org/10.1007/978-3-031-82471-5_5

behalf of the community. The community will then provide two identical he-goats, and lots will be drawn to determine which goat will be offered as a sacrifice for sin, and which will be driven out into the desert carrying the sins of the community (the scapegoat intended for Azazel). The term Azazel is used to indicate both a demon, and a rocky, barren desert both of which are beyond the mercy of God. Uniquely, the Christian gospels are written from the perspective of the innocent victims who are the scapegoats sacrificed to resolve a political and religious crisis in Jerusalem (the trial and execution of Jesus of Nazareth) and the events following that execution (the repression of his disciples and the religious stoning to death of Stephen).

> [...] A scapegoat remains effective as long as we believe in its guilt. Having a scapegoat means not knowing that we have one. Learning that we have a scapegoat is to lose it forever and to expose ourselves to mimetic conflicts with no possible resolution. This is the implacable law of the escalation to extremes. The protective system of scapegoats is finally destroyed by the Crucifixion narratives as they reveal Jesus' innocence, and, little by little, that of all analogous victims. The process of education away from violent sacrifice is thus underway, but it is going very slowly, making advances that are almost always unconscious. [...] Mimetic theory does not seek to demonstrate that myth is null, but to shed light on the fundamental discontinuity and continuity between the passion and archaic religion. Christ's divinity which precedes the Crucifixion introduces a radical rupture with the archaic, but Christ's resurrection is in complete continuity with all forms of religion that preceded it. The way out of archaic religion comes at this price. A good theory about humanity must be based on a good theory about God. [...] We can all participate in the divinity of Christ so long as we renounce our own violence."(Girard, 2010: 97)

An apprehension of the so-called "scapegoat mechanism" and its cultural evolution over millennia provides us with the hermeneutic key for understanding criminal justice, and it's all to frequent tendency not to facilitate healing and forgiveness. Criminal justice is an exemplar *par excellence* of the sacred sacrificial but which no longer works, and yet we continue to flog this dead cultural horse. If the crisis of criminal justice is a crisis of forgiveness, then how rather than renouncing our violence expressed as a demand for justice and satisfaction do we transcend that violence and in ways that does not perpetuate cycles of violence through metaphysical justifications. In Girardian terms, it is time for the *uber-mensch* to plant his feet in the soil of love and to feel and engage with the dirt and risk of contamination.

It is argued by Girard (1987) that as currently used the word scapegoat has three meanings that are frequently confused and need to be separated; biblical, anthropological, and psychosocial. The book of Leviticus (Chapter 16) outlines how on the Day of Atonement two identical goats were to be chosen, one to be sacrificed and the other to be driven into the wilderness. The goat driven out is the scapegoat a term invented by William Tindale in his English translation of the Vulgate (Latin) Bible, from the Old English word "scape" meaning escape; thus, the escaping goat. There are interesting debates concerning the nature and meaning of this ritual and are important in exploring the veracity of Girard's arguments with problems of differentiation in Girard's sources and arguments that need teasing out, but which in my opinion serve to strengthen his argument rather than weaken it. However, as already stated we have the advantage of his full body of work and we can chart his intellectual and personal journey, from the end looking back. It is my view that through analysing the issues we can then look forward in developing an application of his work to practice in the criminal justice system and beyond.

For Girard sacrifice is the main means of communication with the Gods to maintain social order with practices always grounded in violent exclusion. It seems that Girard forgets that on the Day of Atonement that there two goats (see also Gorringe, 1996), one of which is sacrificed, and the scapegoat, or as Douglas calls it "the go-away goat" (Douglas, 2002: 121) which is not attacked, shamed or harmed in any way. This is fundamentally different from the Greek *pharmakós* with Douglas arguing that the concept has moved from a potential animal victim to a real human (scape-person) who will definitely be harmed and possibly killed. She argues that the violent elements not found in the biblical text have perhaps been imported from Greece or Mesopotamia by late interpreter. This is supportive of Girard's view that all Greek thought is structured around *pharmakós*, and if he is correct, and I want to demonstrate that he is, then this has real implications for criminology as the science of expulsion, and the resources that we appropriate for the work of healing and forgiveness. The answer is of course Christianity the very resource that has been expelled by modernists and postmodernists alike. If as Bertrand Russell observed that all Western philosophy is a footnote to Plato, then we can add that all western philosophy is a footnote to the *pharmakós*.

For Western scholars, whether trained in science, social science or the humanities, probably Greek thought is our default position with differences between Plato and Aristotle being the points of departure and divergence. Girard's journey from literary theory to science is read initially through a Greek lens, also of course the writings that became the Christian New Testament were translated into or written in Greek. His mode of inquiry was philosophical but which he soon abandoned, and as others moved into post-structuralism he explored a new framework provided by the Judaeo-Christian scriptures grounded in literary theory. This approach was essential *poietic* opening up new spaces of possibility between the poles of structuralism and post-structuralism. Nonetheless, he arrives at the point of Judaeo-Christian uniqueness through comparison which reveals the differences.

As Mary Douglas[1] (2002) argues the meaning of the term "scapegoat" is contested, with accepted meanings being often at odds with the original biblical account. There is agreement with Gird on the multiplicity of meanings. However, Douglas critiques Girard for his universal application of the scapegoat to mean a variety of persecutory behaviours whose unity and similarities across cultures we grasp intuitively. Girard argues that the scapegoat mechanism as the resolution for mimetic contagion is foundational to all cultures and civilisations, each of which begins with a founding murder (sacrifice). He argues that the mechanism refers to a range of persecutory behaviours found in all cultures that help to bring about or restore social order. This includes the Greek *pharmakós* and the Levitical text concerning the Day of Atonement. In ancient Greece *pharmakós* were the rituals and rites of expulsion of the scum and unwanted of the city, usually from the marginal communities. Persons were processed out of the city while discordant music was playing and they were humiliated and whipped with wild plants as being representative of the evil expelled and carrying the guilt and blame with him.

Girard argues then, that the term "Scapegoat" is as good as any and provides "a rough-and-ready but coherent interpretation not of that ritual alone, but of all others that resemble it (1987:77). Anthropologically, Girard argues that people like Frazer (see e.g. 1950) freely used the term

---

[1] Douglas was herself a practicing Roman Catholic and being intellectually grounded in Durkheim's functionalism sought to understand the development of Christianity within an anthropological context, and she critically engaged with the work of Girard in this respect.

in connection with a number of rituals representing the transference of guilt or sufferings onto a designated victim, usually an animal but sometimes human. The Greek pharmakós (see below) is an example of the latter. Girard observes that the idea of the existence of these distinct categories (presumably in the wake of post-structuralism) has fallen into disrepute and now seen as an outmoded anthropology. The psychosocial meaning is, according to Girard is prevalent in popular culture, where we can clearly identify groups who are wrongly blamed for all kinds of tensions and conflicts in society. At the time of writing the problem of "illegal immigrants" are central to both Donald Trump's presidential election campaign and campaigns by Members of Parliament to become leader of the UK Conservative Party. Crucially though,

> Scapegoating enables persecutors to elude problems that seem intractable. But scapegoating must not be regarded as a conscious activity, based on conscious choice. The very fact that it can be manipulated by people who understand its operation – politicians, for instance – suppose a basic lack of awareness in the passive subjects of such manipulation. Scapegoating is not effective unless an element of delusion enters into it. Proof that we are all prone to that delusion is indirectly accessible through the following paradox: all of us can observe and denounce numerous examples of scapegoating we have personally observed, yet none of us can every identify past and above all, present instances of his or her own involvement in scapegoating. Scapegoat delusion...cannot be assimilated with the "unconscious" of the psychoanalyst, whatever its definition. Some kind of reciprocal suggestion seems to be at working in every form of scapegoating. A social dimension is always present. The victim is often in the singular and the persecutors in the plural. Even when the victims, too, are plural, they are less numerous than their persecutors and, as a result, more or less defenceless. The persecutors are a majority and their victims a minority. Scapegoating in this sense implies a process of displacement or transference that is reminiscent of Freud. But even though it can have sexual connotations,[2] it is not exclusively sexual, as in Freud, and even though it has a linguistic dimension, it is not purely linguistic, as in Frazer. (Girard, 1986a: 74)

---

[2] The issue of sado-masochism is important—in this sense the Nazi high command died as they had lived, and much of the de Sade—Nietzschean genealogy and lives lived falls within this remit too.

Interestingly in this discussion Girard goes onto to outline where he felt Frazer was wrong in his understanding of scapegoating based as it was upon Victorian and colonial prejudices. In this sense, Frazer actually mirrors the bourgeois psychoanalysis of Vienna by claiming that the civilised mind contra the savage mind, through the understanding of words is able to see through its own primitiveness. Thus, lower level and primitive peoples engage in the practices of vicarious suffering for their own individual benefit. This of course is the claim of every elitist in history from Aristotle to Nietzsche. For Aristotle the virtuous man could do no wrong, with anything untoward being due to external and unbearable circumstances and so was in no need of forgiveness (see Pycroft & Bartollas, 2018); for Nietzsche any claim to the contrary was the revenge of the weak against the strong; for Freud and Jung the abreactive process of becoming aware and naming the neurosis that we are suffering from was sufficient to change that neurosis. Like Aristotle, Frazer is saying that modern gentlemen are immune from scapegoating in any form, itself the latest iteration of the "romantic lie" espoused by Rousseau that social order begins in the collective renunciation of violence by the human collective. Peace first, then its corruption through violence, thus the notion of the "noble savage" is born. Girard's position is that the romantic tradition fails to see violence at the inception of culture, and that culture is brought about by exclusion and sacrifice (pharmakós). 'In contemporary debates concerning institutional racism, this lie is espoused through the rhetoric of "a few bad apples" in the organisation rather than racism and the capacity for racism being endemic in the whole organisational culture. Christianity reveals the truth that violent exclusion cannot heal the community, and when violence occurs it becomes concealed in myth and thus Girard rejects Frazer's argument that Christianity is another myth like any other.

Where Frazer and the anthropologists of the time find similarities between religions, Girard finds difference. They saw a whole range of worldwide religious cults based around a sacrificial drama and being positivists assumed that they were all similar with the same explanations. Though he argues that they had no idea why they all seemed to originate in the same type of drama (see Girard, 1986). In this sense, both Judaism and Christianity had the same sacrificial origin as every other religion. But here Girard gives credit to Nietzsche for understanding that facts are meaningless until they are interpreted. In this process by comparing Judaism and Christianity with other myths, an interpretation of the facts provides a very different explanation that is empirically based. The renaissance (romantic) view of Christianity as destroying the classical culture of Greece and Rome (as argued by e.g. Karen Nixey, 2017) is correct, as it seeks to overthrow elitism and violence through love and non-violence and not the imposition of violent metaphysics. The key difference that Girard asserts is that the Christian gospels are written from the perspective of the innocent victims as underdogs and scapegoats ("scum" as the mythical Glaswegian poet Rab C. Nesbitt would say, or *anawim* "the shit of the earth" as St Paul reflects) which is distinct from other ancient myths which conceal the truth of mob violence and is the history of the victors. It is intriguing to think that the small town built on the banks of the Tiber populated by mercenaries and prostitutes which became an imperial city, was given back to those people by Paul of Tarsus in proclaiming the Christian gospel, as the capital of Christendom and consequently the development of Europe.

Nietzsche understood this dynamic perfectly well and was horrified by it. For him, the mob was always justified and therefore innocent, with the victim rightly bearing the guilt (his Dionysus was the antithesis of Christ). His understanding extended to the realisation that the death of Jesus was not sacrificial in these archaic terms and thus undermines the will to power and veracity of human culture. For Nietzsche, the idea of forgiveness as the only way out of this violence was nothing more than *ressentiment,* a slave mentality, and revenge of the weak against the strong (REF). He is aptly described as the last metaphysician with Jean-Luc Nancy (2000) observing that the *Ubermensch* soared so high that he rarely returned to earth. Nietzsche's will to power was an existential option for violence and mastery (see Ruehl, 2018). In the development of Girard's theory, the meeting with Nietzsche's as "Dionysus versus the Crucified" (Girard, 1984) is our useful starting point for criminological debate, particularly as Dragan Milovanovic (2019) argues that Nietzsche is the hero of postmodern thought. In this respect the implications of Nietzsche's thought are taken for granted and the philosophical genealogy of which it is part uncritically accepted. Some evidence for this is found in Ranasinghe's (2020) paper arguing that Nietzsche has been given scant attention in criminology. This is quite remarkable if you consider his influence on Heidegger and the phenomenological tradition and then Foucault and critical theory. I think this demonstrates the ways in which criminology itself conceals its own power and violence with an endless play of theory and multiple meanings at the expense of the truth of suffering and actually doing something about that suffering. This a part of Girard's argument about philosophy that it provides constructs that obscure *haecceity* and the search for truth. It is somewhat ironic that the development of thought that emerged post holocaust could develop both the UN Declaration of Human Rights in 1948, and the development of "theory" as nothing more than interminable language games. The horrors of the twentieth century and the well-intentioned aim of not harming others actually led to the abandonment of others. There is an important ethical argument that in simply remaining and insisting on remaining abstract that the practice of theory is itself violent. For Girard this approach to language games is called "play" because it is without purpose, and when you stop playing you have to commit to action based upon an identification of cause and truth. In this respect the work of Sartre and Camus was highly influential on Girard's thinking (see Adams & Girard, 1993), with the formers system of philosophy, and the latter's humanism both predicated on commitment to the other Both fell out of favour with the postmodernists (and also of course fell out of favour with each other, itself an interesting mimetic rivalry). In criminology it is intriguing (and thankfully important) that Dragan Milovanovic (2014), as one of the foremost advocates of postmodernism has sought a rapprochement between the two cultures with the development of an application to a quantised approach to quantum holography and insights from Lacananian psychoanalysis. I will use this as an important touchstone for the development of my argument with respect to Girard's work and its application to understanding groups and various forms of Durkheimian solidarity, and the relationships between individuals and the group.

CHAPTER 6

Demythologisation: An Anthropology of Forgiveness

Abstract This section will analyse the relationships between demythologisation and re-mythologisation within the context of mechanical and organic solidarity. It will be argued that while the processes of history driven by Judaeo-Christianity have revealed the innocent victims of scapegoating, re-mythologisation is return to violence and an appeal to the myth of mechanical solidarity in the fact of an uncertain world.

Keywords Demythologisation · Re-mythologisation · Mechanical solidarity · Organic solidarity · Populism · Forgiveness · *Imitation Dei* · Romantic lie · Robert Martinson as founding murder of the punitive turn

"Christianity demystifies religion. Demystification, which is good in the absolute, has proven bad in the relative, for we were not prepared to shoulder its consequences. We are not Christian enough. The paradox can be put a different way. Christianity is the only religion that has foreseen its own failure. This prescience is known as the apocalypse. Indeed, it is in the apocalyptic texts that the word of God is most forceful, repudiating mistakes that are entirely the fault of humans, who are less and less inclined to acknowledge the mechanisms of their violence. The longer we persist in our error, the stronger God's voice will emerge from the devastation. [...]

A. Pycroft, *René Girard and Criminal Justice*, Palgrave Pioneers in Criminology, https://doi.org/10.1007/978-3-031-82471-5_6

The Passion unveiled the sacrificial origin of humanity once and for all. It dismantled the sacred and revealed its violence. […] By accepting crucifixion, Christ brought to light what had been 'hidden since the foundation of the world,' in other words, the foundation itself, the unanimous murder that appeared in broad daylight for the first time on the cross. In order to function, archaic religions need to hide their founding murder, which was being repeated continually in ritual sacrifices, thereby protecting human societies from their own violence. By revealing the founding murder, Christianity destroyed the ignorance and superstition that are indispensable to such religions. It thus made possible an advance in knowledge that was until then unimaginable." (Girard, 2010: *x*)

Scapegoating is functional to society and can be read into Durkheim's views on mechanical and organic solidarity, particularly as his view was that the purpose of punishment was to maintain social solidarity through exclusion of the criminal. Therefore, functionally a focus on the criminal for the purposes of group solidarity through passionate denunciation and exclusion provides a ready conveyor belt of scapegoats. Durkheim himself acknowledges that the processes may change in respect of democracy and liberalism but the passions remain the same.

Ignorance and superstition are fundamental to the practices of justice and from a Girardian perspective any *bona fide* criminology, indeed any social science is firstly a victimology as it is Christianity the anti-myth which drives science and progress (see Brague, 2018) as revealed in the judicial trial and execution of Jesus of Nazareth. Jesus the innocent victim reveals the truth of the scapegoating mechanism that underpins social order thus ushering in the modern age. Thus, only a victimology can articulate the desires of criminology to understand crime and our responses to it. Through a "first victimology" that guides our principles we can understand criminology as a part of the problem of crime and social disorder through the failure to acknowledge that the victim is real and not a socially constructed phenomenon. This is a consequence of the failures of not only the decontextualised classicism of "administrative criminology" but a failure of postmodern criminologies. Postmodern fluidity masks ontological violence in the philosophical genealogy of the Marquis de Sade, Nietzsche, Heidegger and Foucault each silences their real victims, whether of their thought and influence or of their physical actions. Each puts cruelty first and if their victims then find their voice and speak out, argue that it is actually they who are the victim. The populist right of politics have brilliantly colonised these powers of deconstruction to undermine institutions for their own narcissistic and solipsistic agendas, and the Left so long desiring to build hegemony for social change has found themselves with no answer, no language with which to respond. The critical tradition has given voice to oppressed and marginalised groups but peace and transformation does not come from demanding harsher penal measures against oppressors. This is the self-defeating logic of "Satan casting out Satan;" When we have been scapegoated we cannot use the same tactics to go after those who have scapegoated us, rather we have to engage in the seemingly impossible work of forgiveness and healing.

Demythologisation and an understanding of the innocence of the victim, and arguments over victim status also bring about re-mythologisation. Re-mythologisation is a return to sacralised violence that we associate with mechanical solidarity. History shows that culture is only wafer thin, and the examples above demonstrate how easy it is to flick this switch, particularly when the perpetrators are developing and deliberately perpetuating (and welcoming) an identity of the scapegoat as the "monstrous other". Their violence has grown out of and emerged from a confluence of historical grievances, and interpretations often with very real experiences of violence, marginalisation, discrimination, poverty and inequality. Violence does not solve these issues, rather leading to an escalation to extremes. Fundamentalism is an attempt at re-mythologisation and the use of scapegoating. What is most terrifying is the conscious choice of people and groups to mobilise these dynamics. At the time of writing, we have seen Hamas' savage attack on Israeli citizens, in the clear knowledge that Israel will not be able to hold back on its retribution. It is effectively demanding the genocide of the Palestinians trapped in Gaza, and Israel has fallen into that trap. The events of 9/11 were designed to achieve similar ends and succeeded far more effectively than al-Qaeda could have imagined, following the unrelated invasion of Iraq. The IRA's bombing campaign on mainland Britain during the 1970s and 1980s was aimed at innocent people to try and grind down support for Northern Ireland remaining part of the UK. Outdoing each other on victim status—the more victims we have the more we can justify retribution—zero sum game leaving everyone blind.

We see this very clearly in current populist politics and particularly the ways in which some Christians have identified with Donald Trump's insurrection (who in Eric Voegelin's phrase, are seeking to "immenatize the eschaton" (2004)). Having victim status (and both Trump and Boris Johnson have claimed that they are victims of witch hunts) however is only half of the story, as we use the transgression of claimed innocence and purity to justify violence against the perpetrators. This generative scapegoating and its escalation to extremes becomes exponential and apocalyptic as we do not accept the peace that is revealed in the Judaeo-Christian narratives culminating in the death and resurrection of Jesus of Nazareth. In offering an anthropology (qua epistemology) of scapegoating and violence in relation to social life Girard grants a phenomenology of the Christian revelation its own integrity, a revelation of truth, with love being the new verb for being. This is expressed as forgiveness (see Pycroft & Bartollas, 2022) as an approach that breaks cycles of violence by not using the logic of the sacred sacrificial to perpetuate cycles of violence.

This raises serious questions concerning what it means to be a practitioner in the criminal justice system, to work on behalf of the state (potentially to be an oath-taker to fulfil a function or office) engaging with the legally justified and bureaucratically administered powers of punishment, deterrence and retribution which do violence to the other. In an applied sense, criminology is the study of criminal justice, and needs to be related to practice therein. While in the various critical, postmodern, and peacemaking perspectives in criminology there is an attempt to address this problem, they themselves are in varying degrees hangovers of the sacred sacrificial. The sacred sacrificial is simply the term for the mechanism that humanity uses to try and control its violence. In both the violence of prehistory (the Hobbesian "war of all" in the state of nature) and the aleatory functions of sacrifice, victims are necessary to maintain systems of law and order. In this very important sense the procedures of law are themselves an heir to sacrifice and raise important questions about justice as a civilising principle (apropos Norbert Elias).

But also, the other key figure is Saul (Paul) of Tarsus a Pharisee who was complicit in the latter execution but following a conversion experience based on unconditional forgiveness becomes the architect of Christianity as Apostle to the Gentiles (see Pycroft in press). In these accounts of violence both Jesus and Stephen forgive their persecutors and refuse to use violence (either from themselves or God) to change their situation. Saul both witnesses (at the execution of Stephen) and experiences (in his conversion and new life) this forgiveness and it thus able to realise their innocence. From this, it follows that Christianity is not a religion but an organising principle that deconstructs the archaic religious and the sacred sacrificial. It demonstrates that violence always comes from people and not from God, and that God reveals to us our own violence as the cause of apocalypse (genocide, global warming, poverty, etc.). We punish ourselves through our own blindness. Reductionist sacrifice is at best an interim and anthropic trade off in an entropic universe of our own imagining. This in the words of Jesus is "Satan casting out Satan". The revelation of the scapegoat mechanism leads to a process of disenchantment with religion (it no longer works), and consequently Girard argues (2001) that we are more concerned with the victim than at any other time in human history. Luther was correct in seeing individuals as neither good nor bad but as both (*simul Justus et peccator*) and our *méconnaissance* coupled with a reductionist mindset means that we have difficulty maintaining this reality. We tend to get shifting and alternate views of one or the other (Žižek (2006) describes this as a parallax view), good or bad rather than holding them in superposition (to borrow a phrase from quantum mechanics—see Pycroft, 2014). For Girard, controversially the solution, is *imitatio Dei* with more Christianity not less.

Other than an argument for the need for *imitatio Dei*, Girard does not provide an alternative vision (I assume that he thought that the Church was that vision, but nonetheless I am not aware that he applied his hermeneutic of suspicion to the actions of the church itself). His unconcealment of the scapegoat and the proclaiming of forgiveness and charity as expressed in Christianity reveals the Judaeo-Christian gospel as one of radical equality before God and people, (so much so that Slavoj Žižek (2009) argues for St Paul as the first Marxist-Leninist). The alternative then, and its application to peacemaking requires further explication. The phenomenology of Girard and also of Heideggeisre read by Vattimo and Zabala (2011) as an interpretation of the meaning of history being one of emancipation from violence. Further, Vattimo sees Heidegger's work as revealing the same victimary mechanism that Girard highlights in Judaeo-Christian scriptures. Both are based on a forgetting e.g. of the founding murder as the ontological reality of all societies (Girard) or identifying beings with objectivity and metaphysics (Heidegger). Through utilising both Girard and Heidegger, Vattimo and Zabala reappraise Christianity to realise that faith in Christ is faith in the weakening of strong structures, namely those that underpin metaphysics (see Harris, 2019). Through weak thought they are seeking to create a postmodern (rather than normative) ethic of weakness through understanding and re-configuring traces and elements from historical thought in accord with postmodern conditions. The question for us, is one of whether historical details matters in respect of e.g. crime, or whether the claims of causality are simply a normative (metaphysical) and descriptive (positivist) retro-engineering of the present to reductively make sense of irruptions that constitute events? This causality post Descartes separates structure and agency creating a space that too readily becomes the place of violence, the natural sacred or the sacred sacrificial that seeks to maintain our total-ising explanation of what, why and how. Strength is variously claimed from both history (expressed as conservatism) and the future (expressed as the revolutionary) and for both the present is expunged by being inter-preted through the lens of time—retribution demands punishment for the crime, rehabilitation demands a new future for criminals. However, the gospel *imitatio Dei*, expressed in the temple theology of the Book of Revelation (also of course known as the Book of the Apocalypse) is one of immanence, where there is no disjunction of structure, agency and time, where Heaven and Earth literally meet (see Barker, 2002). An appreciation of this dynamic and its application to anthropic responsi-bility rather than an abdication to metaphysical judgement (see Pycroft, 2021a) requires a sense-making of the aseity of a God without being (Marion, 2012). Millbank (2006) argues that this Gospel is completely distinct from self-assertion, rivalry and the subtracting of something from others. This subtraction through the demand for sacrifice and carnivals of atrocity (see Miller, 1990) is continued in the criminal justice system as the space of the archaic, and sacred sacrificial (see Pycroft & Bartollas, 2022). We need then to understand not just the theory but the practice of bearing each other's burdens, as our primary choice, rather than our choice being one of condemnation.

He argues that through understanding Jesus' modelling of God's aseity (see below) that we can be freed from our own violence. This is contra the act of (bad) faith in the modern penitentiary where a narrowly focused cognitivism and behaviourism hopes (*sic*) for a pure truth event ex nihilo based on deprivation which will lead (magically) to a "pro social" life for its inmates. Within this argument it is through *méconnaissance* that the self-organising and self-regulating process of violence that is foundational to the origins of human culture and institutions remains hidden or at least partially revealed as a double bind. Girard argues that Christian revelation lifts the veil of méconnaissance so that we now understand the innocence of the scapegoat, whose presumed guilt and our "justified" anger against it has protected us from our own violence. The consequences of this knowledge are that the scapegoating mechanism and the institutions that are built upon it become less effective and leaving us with the problem of how to deal with mimetic crises and our own individual and collective need for vengeance against the other. A reduction in *méconnaissance*, then invites a new perspective on the innocence of scapegoats and our own complicity in violence which can instigate a new space of possibility. As is argued by Dumouchel (2011: 105):

> "...the revelation that is necessary in order to make unanimous victimage impossible is something that will help dissolve individual méconnaissance, something that will make less likely both the actions and representations that come with it. This...is not so much the revelation of the innocence of the victim, as the revelation of the innocence of the other, which is not so much the revelation of the 'sanctity' of the other, as the revelation of his or her radical and fragile humanity. What destroys this méconnaissance is not a belief, a propositional content, but new attitudes like forgiveness and charity extended to all."

Girard fundamentally distinguishes between the archaic mythical structures that have unconsciously evolved to found social order through the aleatory mechanisms of sacrificing scapegoats. Christianity functions as anti-myth, a universal gift to humanity that reveals the scapegoat mechanism and its violence at the heart of all myth and culture. For the traditions and texts that recount myths the sacrificial structure is key but not available to the participants as a conscious *"theme"* (see Alison, 2019) as the knowledge of the reality of random murder is not conducive to social stability. Sacrifice as "theme" emerges in the Hebrew scriptures with stories being written from the perspective of the innocent victim who challenges the fake peace brought about by their murder or exclusion. The originary scene in Christianity is that of Jesus the innocent victim being tortured and crucified by religious and political power and forgiving his persecutors. For Girard this is what distinguishes Christianity from archaic myths and ushers in the modern age, driven and defined by concern for the innocent victim, leading to rationality, science and ultimately atheism. All flourish through the deconstruction of sacred religion with the Jewish and Christian texts as anti-myth forming the hermeneutic key that unlocks the violence of all myth, religion and sacrifice as the truth of those texts.

Take for example the fantasy novel The Lion, the Witch and the Wardrobe,[1] when the four Pevensey children arrive in Narnia and are trying to make sense of what is happening to them and where they should go. They see a Robin, who seems to want them to follow it. There follows a conversation between Peter and Edmund,

> "'...Not so loud' said Edmund; '...but have you realized what we're doing?'
> 'What' said Peter...
> 'We're following a guide we know nothing about. How do we know which side that bird is on? Why shouldn't it be leading us into a trap?'
> "That's a nasty idea. Still - a robin, you know. They're good birds in all the stories I've ever read. I'm sure a robin wouldn't be on the wrong side.'
> (Lewis, 1972: 59)

Peter is countering Edmund's cautious rationality and using myth to interpret myth bordering on what Girard calls the "romantic lie", as Peter never thinks that these stories could be wrong, or unauthentic. Thus, Girard along with the great thinkers of modernity provides us with a hermeneutic of suspicion but rather than dismissing Judaeo-Christianity as just another myth, he argues for deconstructing those myths and revealing their truth to enable a hermeneutic of affirmation. However, the ethical dimension of a hermeneutic of affirmation is not fully developed in Girard's thought. We can identify two themes within this, first, that in line with the psychoanalytic tradition of Freud an assumption that simply becoming aware of my own behaviour leads to personal change of attitudes and behaviours; second that in breaking cycles of violence the need to withdraw from situations of conflict to prevent escalation, suggesting a silence grounded in piety. In response to the first point a long career in working with addictive and compulsive behaviours that society is predicated on demonstrates that most of us understand the need to make change in our lives due to dysfunctions in health and social lives but are unable to do so whether due to our own psychology and/or social barriers and limitations. With respect to the second point neither

---

[1] C.S Lewis was a leading twentieth-century protestant commentator whose children's novels articulated a theology of penal substitution and engaged in a re-mythologizing of Christianity through the lens of Greek thought.

do we necessarily have the ability maybe luxury to withdraw from all situations of conflict, and in this sense, Girard does not provide us with an ethical framework. In his interesting book Robert Doran (2017) looks to the overlap between Girard and Sartre to provide an ethic of conversion, in Sartrean terms this is concerned with authenticity in countering bad faith. I want to take that concept of authenticity and argue for its development through theological rather than philosophical ethics to develop a Girardian contribution to the practice of criminal justice. This approach is predicated on clear differences between scapegoating in Jewish practices and those of the Greek *pharmakós*, the first requiring non-violence, the second requiring the opposite (see below).

The revelation of the innocent victim and the dismantling of archaic religion exposes the apocalyptic consequences that follow. We find ourselves in a double bind, as now we know the scapegoated individual is innocent then we have to do things differently, and build peace through inclusion rather than exclusion. But as Bateson (Steier, 2005: 13) states,

> "The double bind is created in interaction between two or more parties or entities…in a significant non-transient relationship that continues over an extended period, with the same pattern repeated again and again. In this pattern there is a contradiction between messages at different logical levels: a primary injunction and a second conflicting injunction at another level affecting the interpretation of the first. There is some real emotional danger or threat in this situation, no possibility of withdrawing from it, and no possibility of naming the problem"

For Girard the solution of the mimetic crisis is personal sanctity and forgiveness thereby halting an escalation to extremes. Personal sanctity in the institutions of state and society such as the criminal justice system present a double bind for the practitioner. Many people become police officers, probation officers, prison officers out of a sense of wanting to help vulnerable people. Since 2003 I have been directly involved in the teaching and training of probation officers and at induction I always ask why they want to become probation officers. The responses are always the same, with a concern to help vulnerable people, those in trouble with the law and also victims. Over the years I have not heard anybody state the desire to punish, or hold people to account as their motivation and as the discussion continues it becomes apparent that the thought of law and its implementation as violence which people are about to become complicit in, is profoundly disturbing. Herein lies the double bind that is at the heart of some of the problems that institutions are facing such as institutional racism (and other discriminations), violence by professionals against those in their care (prison officers).

What does it mean to be a creative practitioner in criminal justice? The relationship between conformity and creativity is at the heart of all institutions and arguably all of social life. How do we establish, interpret and implement rules and within this context what is the value, purpose and outcome of the individual practitioner and the decisions and actions that they take? Do we want those practitioners to find more creative ways of inflicting pain and suffering on those that we deem to be deserving of it, or do we want our practitioners to be more creative in bringing about change in the lives of those who commit crimes against innocent victims? In reality society seems to demand both and in the unpacking of this double bind the work of René Girard we find some ways of addressing these problems. Girard's thought is focused on the inner workings of violence and the mechanisms of mimesis therein as being foundational to life and social order. It is thus inter-individual and also genetic.

What Girard discovers is the anthropological truth of the Christian gospels demonstrating different ways of being and acting through the practice of forgiveness and peacemaking. Until these prophetic voices are accepted and their messages acted upon they will always be excluded or murdered by the mob justified by *vox populi vox dei*. Critically, those texts do not provide a *deus ex machina* solution as with Greek tragedy to our violence but require us to take responsibility for our own violence and contributions to social violence. We cannot abdicate responsibility to a "God of justice" who demands vengeance for transgression and sin but follow Jesus the god-man in forgiving each other as the model for "good mimesis", social cohesion and human flourishing.

The process of demythologisation in revealing the innocence of the sacrificial victim then leaves us with an ethical dilemma. Do we look for new and non-violent ways of creating social order, or do we seek new justifications and new and unusual ways of doing violence in the name of the greater good? In both the ascendancy of science we have rejected the gospel that gave rise to it as has the critical revolt against modernity. The "Enlightenment" has wrestled mastery over nature from God, and killed him in the process. Nietzsche was correct that if God is dead then we have to act. This then raises critical questions of which God is dead and how ought we to act. Nietzsche, in naming the god who is dead as the God of Judaeo-Christianity, also rejects the actions that arise from a slave mentality of revenge from the weak against the strong as defined by forgiveness.

Robert Martinson (1974) demythologised the prison system in the USA and was effectively killed for speaking the truth of "nothing works" and exposing the lie (myth) of rehabilitation. The suicide of Robert Martinson was in fact a collective murder. In 1980 Martinson jumped from his 9th floor apartment in Manhattan while his teenage son looked on, Martinson was crucified for his research which argued that "nothing works" when it comes to prison rehabilitation programmes, and ushered in the so-called "punitive turn" in criminal justice. Martinson died for telling the truth. Apart from the fact that his work was misrepresented in so far as he argued that there may be effective approaches but that our research methodologies were not good enough to identify them the real truth is that nothing works because it is not designed or intended to work. What prisons and probation services do really well is to exclude, punish, and make money through maintaining a revolving door from which there is no way out. Societies such as in the UK and USA still seek to maintain the myth of rehabilitation (or to be more precise the possibility of operationalising the natural dynamics of desistance) as a consequence of punishment. However, the myth of making good through atonement and giving satisfaction is rendered impossible primarily through the processes of less eligibility and risk assessment and management.

CHAPTER 7

Inter-Individuality and Collective Consciousness: A Quantum Holographic Systems Perspective

Abstract This section will explore the relationships between Girard and Durkheim and their links to Milovanovic's Quantum Holographic Criminology. Contra Milovanovic I argue through utilising *haecceitas* as existing independently of the observer effect that we can learn to see the implicate order as wholeness in flowing movement between both ontology and alterity. The work of society is to facilitate this learning to see and to open up rather than close down opportunities for human flourishing.

Keywords Ontology · Alterity · Implicate order · Quantum Holographic Criminology · Durkheim · Victim as source of order and disorder · Determinism · Agency · Creative practice

It is indicated by Girard (2003) that much of what he discusses in relation to exclusion and sacrifice is to be found either implicitly or explicitly in Durkheim. This appeal to Durkheim is a key link in the genealogy of thought between Girard and quantum holography enabling a discussion of the ways in which the collective acts with unanimity of purpose against individuals or groups. There is significant overlap and agreement between myself and Milovanovic. Whereas he uses the Copenhagen interpretation of quantum mechanics and a Lacanian framework for constituting an inter and intra-subjectively constituted subject (Schema QD), I am arguing from the de Broglie–Bohm model of quantum mechanics and thus suggesting *haecceitas* as consciousness which has the potential to be whole through flowing movement. Every human's *haecceitas*, is an expression of the divinity of Christ the innocent victim, and it is this understanding that eventually leads to ideas of natural rights, liberal democracy, global governance and the UN Declaration of Human Rights (1948), but with a consequent expulsion of the very Christianity that underpins the concepts.

Crucially *haecceitas* is not socially constructed, it exists prior to, and is a realist (positivist) position as it exists independently of the observer. Gilles Deleuze (https://plato.stanford.edu/entries/deleuze/) returned to the concept (originated by Duns Scotus) as the basis for the virtual as the new metaphysics. I concur that potential (ontology) is always realised in relationship (alterity) whereby we become conscious of the self in the other (flowing movement). A reason that theologians talk about creation, is precisely because existence is taken as a gift, and my existence and yours is a gift to the other. Milovanovic's position is as follows (2014:6):

> In understanding agency, or the wherewithal of a person's consciousness, holography theory offers some alternative notions as to how information is encoded, stored, transmitted, and interpreted. In addressing the question of the missing agent in much theorizing in criminology, law and social justice, we will offer a de-oedipalized, quantized version of Jacques Lacan's (a revisionist Freudian psychoanalyst) model of an inter- and intra- subjectively constituted subject. We will call our modified version, schema QD. It is schema QD that when instantiated produces an emitting signature wave that interacts with the "out there" in constituting it where it is, "out there". This follows Bergson's notion that consciousness is not of something, but in something. We are left with the conclusion that everything with which we interact remains with a trace of our signature wave. We are all part of the universe. This is inescapable. We are intricately interconnected with the cosmos. If this is so, dear reader, you can see how thinking in conventional criminology, law and social justice is plainly disconnected and disembodied, leaving the nature of being human a mere shell of what it is and what it can possibly do and become.

In the development of a quantum holographic approach to criminology the work of Dragan Milovanovic (2014) has been ground breaking and provocative. In assessing the status of that work then the review by Raymond Bradley (2015) a pioneer of quantum holography has been useful and helps to understand the complexities of this important field and to seek to develop it further. In his review, Bradley highlights some issues with Milovanovic's concept, two of which are pertinent to my argument: Firstly, he points out that quantum holography is not a branch of quantum physics as implied by Milovanovic; secondly, he has reservations about Milovanovic's use of the concept of the "collapse of the wave function". Both of these issues are linked and stem from Milovanovic's reliance on the Copenhagen version of quantum mechanics (for which he states (Milovanovic, 2014) that there is the most evidence. Bradley (2015) argues firstly that quantum holography has much wider scope than quantum physics as it applies to the macro as well as micro (quantum) worlds for which it can completely and accurately measure communication of energetically encoded information but secondly that human consciousness cannot be reduced to quantum physics vis a vis the collapse of the wave function. I would argue with respect to understanding the relationships between consciousness and matter the de Broglie-Bohm approach to quantum physics may be more helpful to our understanding of consciousness *in something rather than of something* and is of particular relevance to complexity theory, as it gives back reality itself in the form of objectivity, patterns and regularities in the phase space of any given system.

I would highly recommend reading Bradley's (2015) extended review and engagement with Milovanovic's work, as he considerably adds to the learning and development of this approach. So, let us start with a quote linking us back to Durkheim and using this as a point of departure for Girardian thought too:

> Perhaps the most fundamental postulate of sociological theory is the notion that the processes of interaction in all social collectives (groups, organizations, societies) generate an emergent social order—a collective consciousness, which stands above the local exigencies of the psycho-social reality of individuals and embodies a transcendent awareness of the group as a whole. Distributed in all relations throughout the group as a nonlocalized order informing and informed by all interactions, it stands apart as a tacit psychic bond largely beyond conscious awareness of the individual. Describing this order of psychosocial connection one hundred years ago, Emile Durkheim described it in these terms: The collective consciousness is the highest form of the psychic life, since it is the consciousness of the consciousnesses. Being placed outside of and above individual and local

contingencies, it sees things only in their permanent and essential aspects, which it crystallizes into communicable ideas. At the same moment of time that it sees from above, it sees further; at every moment of time it embraces all known reality; that is why it alone can furnish the mind with the moulds which are applicable to the totality of things and which make it possible to think of them...Portending Gabor's discovery of holography in physics, by some thirty years, Durkheim's prescient concept of collective consciousness is the notion of the sociological realm as a holographic informational order. Holographic order is based on a field concept of order in physics. In everyday usage "field" means an area or sphere of operation... This notion of a distinct area within which and throughout which certain activities occur, is also the basis of field concepts in the natural sciences. In physics, a field is an "entity" (usually a force)— nonlocally distributed throughout all or part of a physical system—which operates as a medium or intermediary for interaction between objects or particles (Bradley, 2015: 96)

Within a complex network perspective all of the information is contained within the network and is available (though not necessarily accessed) by every part of the system, and that access to this information is set up by a deterministic pilot wave. This wave is the deterministic attractor that has the capacity to drive both order and disorder, and culturally the victim and information processing about the status of the victim serve this function.

The key to Bohm's argument is;

"...the notion of the enfolded or implicate order. The essential feature of this idea... (is)...that the whole universe is in some way enfolded in everything and that each thing is enfolded in the whole. From this it follows in some way, and to some degree everything enfolds or implicates everything, but in such a manner that under typical conditions of ordinary experience, there is a great deal of relative independence of things. The basic proposal then is that this enfoldment **relationship** (emphasis retained) is not merely passive or superficial. Rather it is active and essential to what each thing is. It follows that each thing is internally related to the whole, and therefore to everything else. The external **relationships** (emphasis retained) are then displayed in the unfolded or implicate order in which each thing is seen, as has already been indicated, as relatively separate and extended, and related only externally to other things. The explicate order, which dominates ordinary experiences as well as classical (Newtonian) physics, thus appears to stand by itself. But actually, it cannot be understood properly apart from its ground in the primary reality of the implicate order. Because the implicate order is not static but basically dynamic in nature, in a constant process of change and development, I called its most general form the holomovement. All things found in the unfolded, explicate order emerge from the holomovement in which they are enfolded as potentialities and ultimately fall back into it. They endure only for some time, and while they last, their existence is sustained in a constant process of unfoldment and re-enfoldment, which gives rise to their relative stable and independent forms in the explicate order" (Bohm, 1990:3).

Within Newtonian/Cartesian dualism there is the assumption that matter occupies discrete space whereas the mind does not. Quantum mechanics challenges that assumption with Bohm's theory developing the argument that the particles of physics have primitive mind-like qualities thus it is not possible to make an absolute distinction between mind and matter. In developing accounts of reality that correspond to contextual, qualitative and connectionist models (contra independent, quantitative and representational models) then Bohmian theory offers real potential. He argues (see Bohm, 1980; Bohm & Hiley, 1987; Bohm, 1990) that particles do follow a well-defined trajectory but that it is always accompanied by a new kind of quantum field. In physics, these quantum fields can be represented as potentials which describe a field as a potentiality, present at each point of space acting on a particle which is at that point. In Newtonian physics the effect is always proportional to the intensity of the field, but in Bohm's theory the quantum potential is dependent only on the form and not the intensity of the quantum field; consequently, even a weak field can strongly affect the particle as can distant environmental factors. This affect from a distance (non-locality) is new, and reintroduces determinism (contra indeterminism) into quantum theory. For Bohm (1990) the key element in understanding this non-localism is the notion of active communication which puts form into the energy (quantum potential) that the particle has. Crucially it is the active communication from within the whole system (quantum field) that gives shape and form to the particle. The ways in which these particles interact is dependent upon the pool of information within the whole system but in ways that cannot be pre-assigned. The quantum potential for a whole system is then non-local and brings about order or form (or "emergence" to use the language of complexity theory).

With respect to what we experience in the classical world of physics as opposed to quantum-level behaviour Bohm (Bohm, 1990) argues for wholeness at the quantum level and objective significance. He argues that active information is the rudimentary mind-like behaviour of matter, given that the essential quality of mind is the activity of form rather than substance. In this theory, active information is both physical and mental in nature in a relationship that continues to exist at infinite levels of subtlety, and our consciousness and thought forms are present at the quantum level. The implications of this approach are profound in which there is no division between mind, matter and consciousness with our whole beings engaging in a "a flux of fundamental participation" (Bohm, 1990: 9). Bohm (1990) argues that both "mind" and "matter" serve only as terms for analysis, which help us to understand things, but cannot be seen as separate substances in interaction with each other, or reduced to serve as a function of the other.

An important contribution to this argument is the work of Penrose and Hameroff (see for example Hameroff, 2012) on the human brain, quantum biology and the rescuing of the concepts of free will and agency from the Cartesian tradition. Their arguments for quantum brain biology address the deterministic problems of (1) reducing conscious-ness and causal agency to neurobiological mechanisms, and (2) that our perceptions which occur after an event are too late for us to respond meaningfully to them (e.g. top tennis players respond to a served ball trav-elling at 120 MPH before they are aware of the need to act); Penrose and Hameroff present a theory of Orchestrated Objective Reduction (Orch OR) in which moments of conscious choice are experienced as a collapse of the quantum wave function in microtubules inside neurons. These microtubules, which are the protein skeletal structures within neurons, provide two or more image states that exist in quantum coherence (super-position) with each other; in this state of pre-conscious superposition there exists a number of possibilities which collapse into an objective reality when a choice is made. Due to the problem of the conscious perception occurring after we have responded to it, consciousness has been seen as illusory. However, the evidence from quantum mechanics and from backward time effects in the brain suggest that quantum state reduction in Orch OR can send quantum information back in time in the order of hundreds of milliseconds. Under the effects of quantum gravity, the moment of choice causes a bulge in the space–time fabric to the smallest possible measure on the Planck scale of 10–33 cm.

This rescues consciousness from being epiphenomenal by providing feedback loops through axonal firings that occur in real time when a conscious choice is made. They argue that if the universe is unfolding rather than human actions occurring due to algorithmic processes, then free will and agency becomes possible; moreover, they argue that their theory is testable and compatible with neuroscience and physics.

Mind, matter and ethics; implications for criminology Paul Cilliers (1998, 2005) argues that complexity theory reveals both the limits of our knowledge and also the irreducibility of meaning but in a non-relativistic way. This limitation is brought about because we inhabit the systems that we study and therefore we can have no absolute and objective knowledge of our lived experience. Meaning and knowledge are contingent and contextual and because it cannot be represented and the context is not transparent we have to choose our hermeneutical frameworks and therefore we cannot escape what is ethical or normative. With respect to both complexity theory and Bohm's work on quantum mechanics we are all co-constitutive of each other's lived experience and therefore have shared responsibility for each other (see Bartollas (2014) for a discussion in respect of peacemaking and constitutive criminologies).

For Bohm (see Bohm, 1968) the implicate order reveals the potential for creativity to social problems whereas the mechanised approach to the universe and the consequent lack of an approach to consciousness and mind has induced at best confusion and at worst a lack of awareness or being in a state of sleep. However, Bohm's work supports much that is progressive within criminal justice practice and rehabilitative social work more broadly. The connectedness of complex systems can lead to constructive change whereas mechanistic approaches to crime, punishment and social problems reduces possibilities for change through closing down the phase space.

This closing down of possibilities within the phase space is best evidenced by the historical selection of a utilitarian version of teleological ethics in politics and economics emphasising the free and calculating individual engaged in the pursuit of pleasure and avoidance of pain. In this Newtonian clockwork universe, the rational, atomised, isolated individual in a state of nature consents with other people to create order; these powerful myths drive the development of liberalism, democracy, human rights, enlightenment, science, humanism, and criminal justice. The consequences for criminal justice (and social policy more broadly) gives rise to the principle of less eligibility. This principle in asserting that if imprisonment is to act as a deterrent then the treatment given to a prisoner should not be greater than that provided to a member of the least significant class in the free society imposes an identity on the poor. The utilitarian argument that the principle is necessary to combat human nature while providing incentives to work (see Sieh, 1989) reaches its denouement over the gates of Auschwitz "Arbeit macht frei" (Work will set you free). In contemporary justice Carlen for example (2015) has been highly critical of the ways in which the class bias effect of less eligibility returns poorer disadvantaged lawbreakers to their place and keeps richer more powerful criminals in theirs, and so undermines any advances. Also, the platonic implication of the "re" in rehabilitation suggests a return to a desirable place/state which is clearly not the case for the majority of criminals (notwithstanding the problem of the arrow of time). More over economic disadvantage is used to economic advantage with prison building, the out sourcing of functions for surveillance and rehabilitation being used to stimulate local economies (see e.g. Blakely, 2005). The principle as applied to the Work House now applies to prison (and to community sentences where it is more often referred to as "less superiority") whereby the prisoners or those on community sentences should not receive a standard of lifestyle or services superior to a non-criminal.

Current approaches to statistically based "frequentist" risk management approaches further contribute to the locking in of retribution and the failures of rehabilitation precisely because these approaches mean that for an individual who has committed a crime the slate cannot be wiped clean because of what they might do in the future requiring information to remain on file.5 Consider the following scenario outlined by a trainee probation officer in England (Clare Robson, 2015:25) when discussing a case that she is supervising in the community:

"I have…used my sessions with Stan to explore his view about identity, boundaries and what situations he finds challenging…it was clear…that he identified himself as a rapper, and a successful upcoming rapper as well. His pride and motivation was evident in his language and recollection of various projects he has worked and the positive feedback he was receiving. Twice during supervision, he burst into song, 'spitting' his new lyrics to give me a flavour of the type of music he was making. His confidence in his identity and ability clearly gave him the type of 'hope' that (desistance theory) suggests offers an offender a stake in their future and increases desistance. In relation to risk registration and assessments probation policy recognises the serious risk of harm posed by perpetrators of domestic violence and as such offenders like

Stan are automatically registered as Medium Risk of Harm at the very least. They cannot be reduced to low risk during the currency of their Order. This poses an ethical dilemma, whereby I expect Stan to demonstrate change but cannot mirror the change to him with a review of his risk. I effectively label him as Medium Risk no matter what he achieves. He successfully completed a domestic abuse programme with excellent feedback from his tutors, he demonstrated a high level of remorse and ended the abusive relationship, but I am still duty bound to keep him registered as Medium Risk."

The justification for this approach as Robson points out, is the consequences of a risk-averse and instrumentalist organisational culture which means that should further offences occur then at least the professional (or rather in these cases the organisation) has demonstrated defensible decision making with respect to the individual concerned. Robson goes onto argue that individual aspiration and potential needed to be routinely worked with and rewarded throughout the supervision of the order, so as to provide the foundations of hope. This an excellent example of the ways in which constructive aspects of rehabilitation are routinely undermined by the wider processes of less eligibility and risk and do not allow for a positive projection of potential for the individual either to themselves or to the wider community.

The evolutionary nature of complex adaptive systems reveals that change can never be retrospective; we can achieve some sense of equilibrium in the phase space (but see the discussion by Needs and Adair-Stantiall (2017) on the fragility of these states) which allows us to function (potentially through quantum brain biology) relative to the arrow of time however we need to return to Gödel and the problem of not being able to access the Platonic realm of objective knowledge. I am arguing that we access new dynamical states (the provision of energy, resources and creativity) through understanding not just that there is no distinction between mind and matter but that the processes of evolution give themselves to us as we emerge with them and feedback into them in the process of becoming. The work of Jean-Luc Marion is particularly insightful here especially his phenomenology of givenness (Marion, 2002) where he argues that "what *shows itself* first *gives itself* (emphasis retained) (Marion, 2002:5). He argues the priority of phenomenology to allow phenomena to reveal themselves and to counter any metaphysics (expressed as ontotheology) by "recognizing, the meaning that the phenomenon itself gives from itself and to itself" (Marion, 2002:9).

CHAPTER 8

Conclusion

Being, Seeing and Changing

Abstract This final section invites us to renounce our own complicity in violence through asking the questions "am I scapegoating?" and how do I become a person for others in my interpretative work as a practitioner.

Keywords Unconscious bias · Scapegoating · Potentiality · Forgiveness · Good mimesis · Bad mimesis · Contagion

The only real and meaningful question that emerges from this whole discussion of Girard's work, is how to renounce my own violence? This is essential if I want to be a peacemaker as violence simply perpetuates and usually escalates violence. The extent to which I am tacitly or overtly engaging in activities that are predicated on *pharmakós and* the perpetuation of *Pólemos* matters e.g. am I scapegoating? As I cannot recognise my own scapegoats, I am reliant on others. However, if I am caught up in cycles of mimetic contagion that justify all kinds of repressions and exclusions against particular groups in the name of justice then this becomes difficult. As a foundational resource, what the Johannine logos reveals is that there is a truth which is embodied love and being, existing prior to my mimetic violence. This space of *haecceity*, of potentiality is forgiveness. The energy that drives the forgiveness that cannot be required is the gift

A. Pycroft, *René Girard and Criminal Justice*, Palgrave Pioneers in Criminology, https://doi.org/10.1007/978-3-031-82471-5_8

of grace (it is interesting that St Paul whose message of grace as transformative energy has been a key focus of continental philosophy in recent years—see Pycroft, 2021).

To paraphrase Bonhoeffer, the truth that both shames and heartens us is to be a man or woman for others. This is the individual practitioner calling out the sacred sacrificial of neoliberal capitalism, bureaucratic rationalism, competition and marketisation, which are indifferent to morality and reform (see Whitehead, 2018). The scapegoat mechanism reveals that the myths and rituals of violence and sacrifice (re)produce state and society, with the mechanisms of justice as bloodstained feedback loops fundamental to social order. Rehabilitation perpetuates these myths. The criminal justice practitioner needs to examine and renounce their own violence but requires a frame of reference within which to understand themselves and the work that they do. This cannot be reduced to a day's training on unconscious bias. It is hard to disagree with Bill Michael, who had to resign from KPMG after saying that "[a]fter every single unconscious bias training that's ever been done nothing's ever improved. So, unless you care, you actually won't change" (https:// www.specta tor.co.uk/ article/ why- unconscious- bias- training- doesn't- work). This training may be a starting point but the reality of police violence and institutional racism in the US and UK are testament to its pervasiveness. It is necessary to constantly ask colleagues and service users the extent to which I/ we are complicit in the dynamics of scapegoating, particularly where there is agreement, consensus and, in legal cases, unanimous verdicts against individuals, which are taken as a good thing because this indicates little room for doubt. The organisations and teams that we work in can all agree on the relative merits of particular individuals or groups of people. However, in the Talmud (the Jewish law) we find a remarkable statement:

> R[abbi] Kahana said: If the Sanhedrin [Jewish court] unanimously find [the accused] guilty, he is acquitted. Why? – Because we have learned by tradition that sentence must be postponed till the morrow in hope of finding new points in favor of the defense. But this cannot be anticipated in this case. (cited by Glatt, 2013: 322)

There is extensive debate concerning the meaning of this paradoxical statement, with Glatt (2013) offering the following observations. First, the nineteenth-century scholar Zvi Hirsh Chajes argues that it is the role of the Sanhedrin to make an impossible argument, particularly because in the face of a lack of dissenting opinion, collusion must be suspected; hence, they are not doing their job properly as they are not making the impossible arguments, and the charge should be dismissed. In fact, the basis for admission to the Sanhedrin is the ability to provide "a cogent, logical argument for an impossible factual scenario. The judge must prove that a certain dead animal, ritually impure according to the explicit text of the Bible, is actually ritually pure according to Jewish law" (Glatt, 2013): 324). Likewise, in the sixteenth century Judah Loew argued that the role of the Sanhedrin is to search for evidence of innocence rather than guilt and to be committed to finding merit in the defendant rather than being concerned with punishment. For Loew, the integrity of the court as one of righteousness that frees rather than punishes innocent people is the priority (this is a statement of the priority of due process models of justice). There are further views concerning the nature of punishment as being spiritually cleansing, with Menachem Mendel Morgenstern arguing that punishment is the mode of forgiveness. In this approach, the role of the Sanhedrin is to help a person to realise that they have done wrong and to regret their actions. A unanimous verdict would bring about this understanding to the offender, obviating the need for punishment.

As Girard demonstrates clearly change, whether for good or bad is contagious. Simply to will our own actions as a universal good in the Kantian sense can lead to the perversity of de Sade willing violence in the name of individual pleasure and a right to that pleasure. This is the trap that much postmodern thought falls into and in criminology reaching an apotheosis with Katz's (1988) book where we are invited to be seduced by and presumably enjoy pruriently the violence committed to others. This perpetuation of cruelty first and its genealogy since de Sade, via Nietzsche, Heidegger and Foucault needs to be transformed through love.

It occurred to me that we have no institutions committed to inclusion, whereas we have many dedicated to exclusion through various means. In the UK, the closest that we have is the National Health Service (NHS) which is universal and free at the point of delivery. Public health approaches are key parts of universal and equitable health delivery and reduce the necessity of trying to change behaviour through punishment and deterrence. There are powerful arguments for decriminalising all currently illicit drug use, for removing treatment programmes for mental health from the criminal justice system and treating sexual abuse against children as a public health issue (see the pioneering work of the Gracewell Clinic and Lucy Faithfull Foundation).

Addressing these issues and ways of thinking is critical for people working in the criminal justice system (and beyond) where bureaucratic routinisation of decision-making and activities obscures the violence done to individuals, their families and communities. Take one example that in England and Wales the majority of people on probation, being supervised in the community are returned to prison for technical breaches of their orders rather than having committed another crime (Prison Reform Trust, 2024). Having been late for an appointment, failing drug tests (and most criminals do not have the advantages of elite athletes to challenge those test findings), not notifying a change of address, etc. can all lead to recall. We know from the data that particular groups are treated more harshly by the system that is made up of people. So, recalling Robert Cover's argument (page 15) we need to understand our own capacity for discrimination and we all have that capacity.

In Redemptive Criminology (Pycroft and Bartollas, 2022) we outlined our backgrounds as being a key part of our hermeneutical narratives of self. I grew up in an entirely white semi-rural community in southern England, made up largely of working class and lower middle-class people. The culture was inherently racist, sexist and classist, and I still hear those unbidden voices that come out of my past. I have been fortunate in my education, my work and my training. Working in social work and the importance of anti-discriminatory practice has been key, as has developing therapeutic alliances in casework and group work. Clinical supervision is essential. Most professional groupings though do not get these supports, and they should. However, I am increasingly of the view that we need "liturgies of the everyday" in organisations that allow us to share, discuss and receive support independently of management and performance frameworks to enable an exploration of who we are. This maybe an increased role for chaplaincy, though this does not have to be "religious". It may simply be the sharing of a meal, a discussion about difficult feelings generated by difficult work. I always say to trainee probation officers to pay most attention to the cases that you find most difficult as these tell you the most about yourself.

Ultimately whatever the evaluation of Girard's work, this consciousness of self, and my complicity and capacity for change and what to do about it, is a series of questions both simple and powerful that are worth addressing. Interestingly by reading the resources that enable me to make sense of myself from both present and past, much is revealed that has been obscured by Enlightenment and post-Enlightenment thought. In addressing the crises of criminal justice as symptomatic of wider concerns that can only be described as apocalyptic, then I recommend the study of Girard as a way of cleaning our lens in helping us to see and be for others.

References

Adams, R., & Girard, R. (1993). Difference, sacrifice: A conversation with René Girard. *Religion & Literature, 25*(2), 9–33.

Alison, J. (2003). *On being liked*. Darton, Longman and Todd.

Alison, J. (2019). Eucharist and sacrifice: The transformation of the meaning of sacrifice through revelation. In J. Alison & W. Palaver (Eds.), *The Palgrave handbook of mimetic theory and religion* (pp. 201–207). Palgrave Macmillan.

Améry, J. (1999). *At the mind's limits*. Granta.

Arendt, H. (2006). *Eichmann in Jerusalem: A report on the banality of evil*. Penguin Classics.

Armour, M., & Umbreit, M. (2005). The paradox of forgiveness in restorative justice. In E. Worthington (Ed.), *Handbook of forgiveness* (pp. 449–503). Routledge.

Atlan, H. (2013). *The sparks of randomness Volume 2: The atheism of scripture*. Stanford University Press.

Badiou, A. (2003). *Saint Paul: The foundation of universalism*. Stanford University Press.

Bartollas, C. (2014). Constituting the system: Radical developments in post-Newtonian society. In A. Pycroft & C. Bartollas (Eds.), *Applying complexity theory: Whole systems approaches to criminal justice and social work* (pp. 269–286). Policy Press.

Bash, A. (2015). *Forgiveness: A theology*. Cascade Books.

Blakeley, C. (2005). *America's prisons: The movement toward profit and privatization*. Brown Walker Press.

Bloom, A. (1988). *The closing of the American mind*. Simon and Schuster.

Bohm, D. (1968). On creativity. *Leonardo, 1*(2), 137–149.

© The Editor(s) (if applicable) and The Author(s), under exclusive license to Springer Nature Switzerland AG 2025
A. Pycroft, *René Girard and Criminal Justice*, Palgrave Pioneers in Criminology, https://doi.org/10.1007/978-3-031-82471-5

Bohm, D. (1980). *Wholeness and the implicate order*. Routledge.

Bohm, D., & Hiley, B. (1987). An ontological basis for the quantum theory. *Physics Reports, 144*, 323–348.

Bohm, D. (1990). A new theory of the relationship of mind and matter. *Philosophical Psychology, 3*(2), 1–14.

Bohm, D. (2000). *Wholeness and the implicate order*. Routledge.

Bradley, R. (2015). Bonds and quanta: Commentary on quantum holographic criminology. *Journal of Theoretical and Philosophical Criminology, 7*(2), 95–136.

Brague, R. (2018). *The kingdom of man: Genesis and the failure of the modern project*. University of Notre Dame Press.

Bull, M. (ND). Cultural criminology: The work of Rene Girard. Retrieved June 12, 2023, from https://www.anthro.ox.ac.uk/sites/default/files/anthro/doc uments/media/jaso19_3_1988_265_274.pdf

Bull, M. (1994). Oedipus was innocent. *London Review of Books, 16*(5).

Bull, M. (2019). *On mercy*. Yale University Press.

Burke, K. (1954). *Permanence and change: An anatomy of purpose*. University of California Press.

Butler, B. (1981). Foreword. In J. P. de Caussade (Eds.), *The sacrament of the present moment* (pp. 7–8).

Carlen, P. (2013). Against rehabilitation: For reparative justice. *Criminal Justice Matters, 91*(1), 32–33.

Cassirer, E. (1967). *An essay on man*. Yale University Press.

Christie, N. (1977). Conflicts as property. *British Journal of Criminology, 17*(1), 1–15.

Cilliers, P. (1998). *Complexity and postmodernism: Understanding complex systems*. Routledge.

Cilliers, P. (2005). Complexity, deconstruction and relativism. *Theory, Culture, Society, 22*(5), 255–267.

Collini. S. (2013). Leavis V Snow: The two-cultures bust up 50 years on. In *The Guardian 16th August*

Cover, R. (1995). Violence and the word. In M. Minow, M. Ryan, & A. Sarat (Eds.), *Narrative, violence and the law: The essays of Robert Cover* (pp. 203–238). Michigan University Press.

Crewe, D. (2019). Blame, responsibility and peacemaking. *Journal of Theoretical and Philosophical Criminology, 11*(1), 1–17.

de Castro Rocha, J. C. (2019). *Shakespearean cultures: Latin America and the challenges of mimesis in non-hegemonic circumstances*. Michigan State University.

Derrida, J. (1968). Plato's Pharmacy. *Tel Quel, 32*, 33.

DeValve, M. (2015). *A different justice: Love and the future of criminal justice*. Carolina Academic Press.

Dingwall, G., & Hillier, T. (2015). *Blamestorming, blamemongers and scapegoats: Allocating blame in the criminal justice process.* Policy Press.

Doran, R. (2017). *The ethics of theory: Philosophy, history, literature.* Bloomsbury.

Dumouchel, P. (2011). De La Méconnaissance. *Lebenswelt, 1,* 97–111.

Dupuy, J. P., & Anspach, M. (1994). The self-deconstruction of convention. *SubStance, 23*(2), 86–98.

Dumouchel, P., & Wilmes, A. (2017). René Girard and philosophy: An interview with Paul Dumouchel. *The Philosophical Journal of Conflict and Violence, 1*(1). https://doi.org/10.22618/TP.PJVC.20171.1.95003

Douglas, T. (1995). *Scapegoats: Transferring Blame.* Routledge.

Douglas, M. (2002). The go-away goat. In R. Rendtorff & K. Kugler (Eds.), *The book of Leviticus: Composition and reception* (pp. 121–141). Brill Publishing.

Eagleton, T. (2003). *After theory.* Penguin Books.

Eagleton, T. Culture and barbarism: Metaphysics in a time of terrorism. Commonweal 136/6 (27 March 2009).

Foucault, M. (1977). *Discipline and punish: The birth of the prison.* Allen Lane.

Frazer, J. (1950). *The golden bough.* Macmillan.

Friedland, P. (2014). *Seeing justice done: The age of spectacular capital punishment in France.* Oxford University Press.

Fromm, E. (2001). *The fear of freedom.* Routledge.

Girard, R. (1976). Superman in the underground: Strategies of Madness-Nietzsche, Wagner, and Dostoevsky. *Comparative Literature, 91*(6), 1161–1185.

Girard, R. (1984). Dionysus versus the crucified. *MLN, 99*(4), 816–835.

Girard, R. (1986a). Nietzsche and Contradiction. *Stanford Italian Review, 6*(1–2), 51–65.

Girard, R. (1986b). *The scapegoat.* Johns Hopkins Press.

Girard, R. (1987). Generative scapegoating. In W. Burkett, R. Girard, & J. Smith (Eds.), *Violent origins: Ritual killing and cultural formation* (pp. 73–148). Stanford University Press.

Girard, R. (1988). *Violence and the sacred.* Athlone Press.

Girard, R. (2003). *Things hidden since the foundation of the world.* Continuum.

Girard, R. (2007). *Evolution and conversion: Dialogues on the origins of culture.* Continuum.

Girard, R. (2001). *I see Satan fall like lightening.* Gracewing.

Girard, R. (2010). *Battling to the end: Conversation with Benoît Chantre.* Michigan State University Press.

Girard, R. (2023). The founding murder in the philosophy of Nietzsche. In C. Haven (Eds.), *René Girard all desire is a desire for being: Essential writings* (pp. 21–40). Penguin Classics.

Glatt, E. (2013). The unanimous verdict according to the Talmud: Ancient law providing insight into modern legal theory. *Pace International Law Review Online Companion, 3*(10), 316–335.

Gorringe, T. (1996). *God's just vengeance*. Cambridge. University Press.

Gorringe, T. (2002). The prisoner as scapegoat: Some skeptical remarks on present penal policy. In T. O'Connor & N. Pallone (Eds.), *Religion, the community and the rehabilitation of criminal offenders* (pp. 249–257). Haworth Press.

Gorringe, T. (2021). Interpreting the cross: Religion, structures of feeling, and penal theory and practice. In A. Millie (Ed.), *Criminology and public theology: On hope, mercy and restoration* (pp. 93–110). Bristol University Press.

Hameroff, S. (2012). How quantum brain biology can rescue conscious free will. *Frontiers in Integrative Neuroscience, 6*(93), 1–17.

Harris, M. (2019). Gianni Vattimo. *Internet Encyclopaedia of Philosophy*.

Haven, C. (2018). *Evolution of desire: A life of René Girard*. Michigan State University Press.

Heim, S., & M. (2006). *Saved from sacrifice: A theology of the cross*. Eerdmans Publishing.

Houston, S., & Swords, C. (2022). Critical realism, mimetic theory and social work. *Journal of Social Work, 22*(2), 345–363.

Husserl, E. (2017). *Ideas: General introduction to pure phenomenology*. Matino Fine Books.

Johnsen, W. (2019). Introduction to the thought of René Girard. In *Violence and the sacred in the ancient near east: Girardian conversations at Çatalhöyük* (pp. 28–38).

Jun, N. (2007). *Toward a Girardian politics*. https://www.researchgate.net/publication/252934438_Toward_a_Girardian_Politics

Katz, J. (1988). *Seductions of crime*. Basic Books.

Kearney, R. (1999). Aliens and others: Between Girard and Derrida. *Cultural Values, 3*(3), 251–262.

Levi, P. (1985). *The periodic table*. Abacus Books.

Lewis, C. S. (1972). *The lion, the witch and the wardrobe*. Puffin Books.

Macksey, R., & Donato, E. (Eds.). (1972). *The structuralist controversy: The languages of criticism and the sciences of man*. The Johns Hopkins Press.

Marion, J., & L. (2002). *Prolegomena to charity*. Fordham University Press.

Marion, J., & L. (2012). *God without being*. University of Chicago Press.

Martinson, R. (1974). What works? Questions and answers about prison reform. *The Public Interest, 35*, 22.

Milbank, J. (2006). *Theology and social theory: Beyond secular reason* (2nd ed.). Blackwell.

Miller, W. (1990). Carnivals of atrocity: Foucault, Nietzsche, Cruelty. *Political Theory, 18*(3), 470–491.

Milovanovic, D. (2014). *Quantum holographic criminology: Paradigm shift in criminology law and transformative justice.* Carolina Academic Press.

Milovanovic, D. (2019). *Postmodern criminology.* Routledge.

Murji, K. (2019). Scapegoating. In MaClaughlin and Muncie Sage D*ictionary of criminology*

Nancy, J. L. (2000). *Being singular plural.* Stanford University Press.

Needs, A., & Adair-Stantiall, A. (2017). The social context of transition and rehabilitation. In G. Akerman, A. Needs, & C. Bainbridge (Eds.), *Transforming environments and rehabilitation: A guide for practitioners in forensic settings and criminal justice* (pp. 31–62). Taylor and Francis.

Nietzsche, F. (1974). *The gay science.* Random House.

Nixey, K. (2017). *The darkening age: The Christian destruction of the classical world.* Macmillan.

Ortolano, G. (2005). F.R. Leavis, Science and the abiding crisis of modern civilization. *Hist.Sci xliii*: 1–25

Pepinsky, H. (2006). *Peacemaking: Reflections of a radical criminologist.* University of Ottawa Press.

Pycroft, A. (2010). *Understanding and working with substance misusers.* Sage.

Pycroft, A. (2018). Consciousness in rather than of: Advancing modest claims for the development of phenomenologically informed approaches to complexity theory. *Journal of Theoretical and Philosophical Criminology, 10*, 1–20.

Pycroft, A., & Bartollas, C. (2018). Forgiveness as potentiality in criminal justice. *Critical Criminology, 26*, 233–249.

Pycroft, A., & Bartollas, C. (2022). *Redemptive criminology.* Bristol University Press.

Pycroft, A. (2020). Between Athens and Jerusalem in peacemaking criminology: The importance of weak and marginal positions. *Journal of Theoretical & Philosophical Criminology, 12*, 188–199.

Pycroft, A. (2021a). St Paul among the criminologists. In A. Millie (Ed.), *Public theology and criminology: On justice, mercy and forgiveness* (pp. 71–91). Bristol University Press.

Pycroft, A. (2021b). The surveillance of substance misuse and the drug use industry. In B. Arrigo & B. Sellers (Eds.), *The pre-crime society: Crime, culture and control in the ultramodern age.* Bristol University Press.

Pycroft, A., & Bartollas, C. (Eds.). (2014). *Applying complexity theory: Whole systems approaches to criminal justice and social work.* Policy Press.

Quinney, R. (1991). The way of peace: On crime, suffering and service. In H. Pepinsky & R. Quinney (Eds.), *Criminology as peacemaking* (pp. 3–13). Indiana University Press.

Quinney, R. (1995). Socialist humanism and the problem of crime; Thinking about Erich Fromm in the development of critical/peacemaking criminology. *Crime, Law and Social Change, 23*(2), 147–156.

Ranasinghe, P. (2020). Friedrich Nietzsche, *On the genealogy of morals* and criminology. *Theoretical Criminology*. https://doi.org/10.1177/136248062097 7853

Ricoeur, P. (2004). *Memory, history, forgetting*. University of Chicago Press.

Rieff, P. (2007). *Charisma: The gift of grace, and how it has been taken away from us*. Pantheon Books.

Robson, C. (2015). *A critical analysis of the role of probation in improving outcomes for gang members and violent offenders*. Unpublished Work Based Learning Project.

Ruehl, M. (2018). In defence of slavery: Nietzsche's dangerous thinking. *The Independent* 2nd January

Shullenberger, D. (2021). The violence of institutions, or Girard avec Foucault' Outsidertheory.com/The violence of institutions, or Girard avec Foucault accessed 9/6/23

Sieh, E. (1989). Less eligibility: The upper limits of penal policy. *Criminal Justice Policy Review, 3*, 159–183.

Steier, F. (2005). *Gregory Bateson: Essays for an ecology of ideas*. Imprint Academic.

Thomas, K. (1978). *Religion and the decline of magic*. Peregrine Books.

van Dijk, J. (2008). In the shadow of Christ? On the use of the word 'victim' for those affected by crime. *Criminal Justice Ethics, 27*(1), 13–24.

Vattimo, G., & Zabala, S. (2011). *Hermeneutic communism: From Heidegger to Marx*. Columbia University Press.

Vattimo, G., & Girard, R. (2006). *Christianity, truth and weakening faith: A dialogue*. Colombia University Press.

Voegelin, E. (2004). *Science, politics and gnosticism*. ISI Books.

Whitehead, P. (2018). *Demonising the other: The criminalisation of morality*. Policy Press.

Wolterstorff, N. (1994). Tertullian's enduring question. In *The Cresset Trinity Special Issue Lilly Fellows Program in Humanities and Arts* (pp. 5–17).

Young, J. (2012). *The criminological imagination*. Polity.

Žižek, S. (2009). *Violence*. Profile Books.

Žižek, S. (2011). The fear of four words: A modest plea for the Hegelian reading of Christianity. In C. Davis (Ed.), *The monstrosity of Christ: Paradox or dialectic* (pp. 24–109). Massachusetts Institute of Technology Press.

INDEX